BARACK OBAMA
VS
THE BLACK HEBREW ISRAELITES

Introduction to the History & Beliefs of
1West Hebrew Israelism

LIMITED PRE-RELEASE ABRIDGED EDITION

Vocab Malone

Phoenix, Arizona USA

Printed in the United States of America.

Cover design and layout by Nathan Scherer
http://www.nathansmart.com.

Photography by The Microscopic Giant
https://www.flickr.com/photos/muggypython/.

Printing and publishing by LionHouse Publishing.

Author photo by Daniel Lovelace.

Co-editing by Ashley Cnossen.

TO

Malachi Cruz
Luke Apollos
Micah Ezra
Leo Judah Josiah

οὐ γὰρ ἐλάβετε πνεῦμα δουλείας πάλιν εἰς φόβον ἀλλὰ ἐλάβετε πνεῦμα υἱοθεσίας ἐν ᾧ κράζομεν· αββα ὁ πατήρ

~ Romans 8:15 ~

TABLE OF CONTENTS

*"2008 was the year I began to watch YouTube videos with my father of Hebrew Israelites dressed in thrifty clothes that looked like they'd been pulled out of a dumpster. The videos we usually watched were of a camp consisting of all men, as most are. These b******* stood on the corners of New York streets, and videoed themselves cursing out white people and calling President Obama a devil".*

– Hannah Spivey, *Why I Abandoned the Hebrew Israelite Religion: A Memoir/Self-Help Guide*

INTRODUCTION

1981 - one year after Luke Skywalker discovered Darth Vader was his father; one year before Snake-Eyes and Cobra Commander graced Toys 'R' Us shelves; the year a 21-year old college student arrived in New York City to attend Columbia University. The young student's name: Barack Obama (his friends called him Barry). In 2016, NetFlix released *Barry*, a film chronicling young Obama's search to find where he fits in this world. The film shows the man who would later become the President of the United States playing basketball, learning, studying, arguing, partying, reading, dating, eating, wondering and wandering. Obama transferred from Oxy to Columbia in fall 1981. His apartment was on West 109th Street in Harlem, between Amsterdam and Columbus – very close to the original 1West Hebrew Israelite school.

In one scene, young Obama walks through Harlem. The camera focuses on a man yelling at pedestrians through a microphone. As Obama engages him, the man reveals himself to be a "Hebrew Israelite". Hence, the title of this pre-release book: *Barack Obama vs. The Black Hebrew Israelites*. The *Barry* movie debate scene is the launching pad from which we explore the basics of Hebrew Israelism – its history, doctrine and practice. This unorthodox approach will hopefully shed light on a massively confusing and mysterious subject: the religion of Hebrew Israelism.

A NOTE ON THE PHRASE "BLACK HEBREW ISRAELITES"

Most modern "Hebrew Israelites" view the designation "Black Hebrew Israelite" as a slur (I wonder if they would like "Hebrew IsraeLITE" better?). I will not delve into the reasons here but I will point out this is a newer sensitivity. This used to be a name they would call themselves but now claim is racist. The Internet digital archiving service known as "The Wayback Machine", displays older "Hebrew Israelite" websites where they *refer to themselves* as "Black Hebrew Israelites" (Christian apologist "Faithful to God" of Soldiers of God has examples on file). Two books released in 2017 by "Hebrew Israelite" authors bear this designation in their titles: *The Great Awakening of the Black Hebrew Israelites ... in these Last Days* by Jacqueline A. French and *Black Hebrew Israelites Scriptures: - The Covenant: For Believers in the Old Testament Only* by Teresa M. Walker and Yshy Yahazy'Ahl. Some "Hebrew Israelite" leaders still use this phrase as well. For example, in a promo video released June 7, 2017 titled "The Bible vs. Ministers" on IUIC's Facebook page, Nathanyel tells followers to "stop listening to unlearned Black Hebrew Israelites" (1:20 mark).

I typically use "Hebrew Israelites," and almost always in quotation marks. Why? There are no compelling reasons to believe that most self-identified "Hebrew Israelites" are truly Hebrew or Israelite – ethnically, nationally, or religiously. Quotation marks can denote a contentious phrase; i.e., they call themselves "Hebrew Israelites" but employ it in a non-standard way. The term "Hebrew Israelite" should be used cautiously; for it is not prudent to assume all self-designations have epistemic warrant (see: Bruce Jenner and Rachel Dolezal). It's best to utilize a term I first heard Dr. James White: *Hebrew Israelism.*

A NOTE ABOUT THE APPROACH AND STYLE OF THIS BOOK

This book is *not* directed at professional academics. It is not designed to conform to all the rule and regulations of a dissertation. This is not to say it is inaccurate or careless, or that it contains no trappings of a professional research paper. This booklet occasionally includes academic jargon. However, an average adult should feel comfortable comprehending this small work; it is designed to communicate effectively with a serious and curious lay reader.

This small work is undoubtedly eclectic in its approach and style, as most works in the field or urban apologetics need to be. If you are uneasy about a publication switching from a bible passage to citing an academic journal then referencing pop culture and then casually using slang terms, then it may take a chapter to adjust to the writing style. Once you accept the unorthodox approach, I trust you will find it engaging, enjoyable, and even entertaining. Be flexible. Eventually, you will learn to shift rapidly from second to fourth gear and back down to first.

The reader must also be aware this work is *not* an all-out refutation of Hebrew Israelism. The subtitle is "an introduction to the history and beliefs of 1West Hebrew Israelism"; it is a basic introduction. There are small moments of counter apologetics; that is not the bulk of the work, though. Hebrew Israelism is such a mysterious religion that a large amount of ground work must be done. A future edition or sequel to this work will include more interaction with the Scripture and history 1Westers abuse. This means a future edition will include more refutation. That is why this version says "abridged" version – there is a longer version of this edition. After feedback and more editing, I hope to release that material as well.

Please appreciate that massive nature of this topic and understand this is only the beginning of what needs to be a massive apologetic enterprise. With that said, enjoy and *soli deo Gloria*!

"This guy's something else. He's an Israelite, anyway. I don't know what his problem is. He's an Israelite, anyway. Actually, he sounds like an Israelite. He's supposed to be Sicilian; if he's Sicilian, then he's gotta be an Israelite. There's a couple of pictures of him with a big bushy afro, man. ... According to what I understand, Vocab Malone is a Sicilian, so he's most likely an Israelite. There's a picture of him playing basketball, I guess in college or high school, that's something that Jake like to do. He's a Christian rapper – he's a rapper, right? That's' something that Jake like to do. Alright, so from all what I see, he's gotta be an Israelite! He's gotta be an Israelite. So he's fulfilling prophecy. That's why he's on the comment board right now."

– Tahar of the Great Millstone Israelites (SOURCE: YouTube video called "Vocab (Malone) Doesn't Understand the Scriptures", July 4, 2016).

ENGAGING 1WEST HEBREW ISRAELISM

The "Hebrew Israelites" are a religious group growing in visibility, activity and influence in many urban areas. I have received dozens of calls since early 2016, all reporting an increased flurry of "Hebrew Israelite" activity. Self-reports, although often exaggerated, match this observation. According to a current online list, ISUPK (Israelite School of Universal Practical Knowledge) claims at least 20 US schools and one in the UK. Their influence is spreading beyond mere geographic boundaries; ISUPK advertises a Spanish-language hotline and a prison ministry program. A Texas prison chaplain told me he observes Hebrew Israelism displacing the Nation of Islam as the fastest-growing religion in the Houston prison system.

Slowly, media outlets are taking note: Viceland TV debuted *Hate Thy Neighbor* in January 2017. The synopsis for Episode 2 ("Hunting the White Devil") is "Jamali goes to Harlem, NY to meet black separatists".[1] ISUPK and other "Hebrew Israelite" groups are the episode's focal point (the episode contains foul language and crude speech but I still highly recommend it for educational purposes, as it is eye opening to the average person).

The main venues "Hebrew Israelites" proselytize are city blocks. The average "Hebrew Israelite" Annoy-Your-Neighbor Starter Kit includes a mic, a platform, a few offensive poster boards, a tattered KJV, a red Apocrypha, and a busy street corner. Street teaching (adherents call it "setting up camp" or "going to camp") is becoming part of the urban landscape in more and more cities. For example, the 2016 crime-thriller flick *Triple 9* features a brief scene where "Hebrew Israelites" are yelling at Woody Harrelson.[2]

Online videos are the messaging vehicles of choice (witness the constant increase in YouTube uploads by these groups!). Simultaneously, there has been a marked increase in production quality. Some camps work diligently on visual branding and in professional presentation. A perfect example is the camp known as Israel United in Christ. The video to their infamous diss track, "Purple Reign", demonstrates the artistic and professional capabilities of the group (everything is done "in-house").

There has been an increase in self-published books, music, and social-media graphics (memes, illustrations, charts, etc.), adding to a media proliferation of their message on a scale not previously observed. "Hebrew Israelites" produce (and believe) so much "meme theology", I know an apologist who began a Facebook page strictly dedicated to debunking their memes!

Some Christians look at these developments and may feel they do not know how to engage or even what to think about these groups. The church of Jesus Christ needs to figure it out – it's important! The rise of Hebrew Israelism affects the global church of Christ. Hebrew Israelism doctrines especially affect Christians in large cities. The spread of

Hebrew Israelism impacts families as well. Allow an anecdote: while visiting a "Hebrew Israelite" message board, a recent convert asked the forum if he had to divorce his wife because she was white (an "Edomite"). The unanimous answer: yes, he needed to divorce her. Disturbing testimonials are coming out on this heartbreaking trend, such as interviews with people who had their family ripped apart due to 1West doctrine.[3]

This movement especially affects the traditional black church, but also Christian congregations made up of diverse peoples. The challenge of "alternative spiritualties" competing for the "souls of black folk" (a phrase coined by WEB DuBois) comes at a crucial time, when the historically black church faces multiple challenges – a few challenges are millennial attitudes and habits, gentrification and the increasing secularization of the culture.[4] The black Christian community has been negatively affected by the mini-exodus of young black men from their midst. Very few apologetic resources are designed to help black Christians who seek to give wise answers to "Hebrew Israelites". Per 1 Peter 3:15, the time is now for apologetically-minded Christians to write, speak, and teach the truth about Hebrew Israelism.

To reiterate the problem: there are no apologetic books dedicated to Hebrew Israelism in the light of Christian doctrine (and only a handful of scattered online articles).[5] There is a void. We need to properly explain Hebrew Israelism before we can properly refute their teachings. People must understand what they are actually arguing for and against. Furthermore, vulnerable (and those already damaged by Hebrew Israelism) Christians need to be protected and defended. God's people need practical answers to these pressing questions as we have real life evangelistic encounters with the lost. I pray this booklet is part of the beginning of this task. I hope it's a small contribution towards a much larger project.

ALL PEOPLES AND ALL NATIONS MEANS JUST THAT

In Matthew 28:19-20, Jesus lays out the Great Commission. It includes the command to "make disciples of all nations". The Greek word translated "nations" is ethnos, connoting peoples (as in "all peoples") or a people group. Black and Hispanic Americans both constitute people groups. Part of fulfilling the Great Commission is to ensure there are disciples from all peoples. Since hindrances exist which block certain people groups from believing the truth of the gospel message, disciples of Christ should labor to remove said hindrances. Hebrew Israelism is acting as a serious hindrance towards young black and brown men from coming to Christ.[6] Evangelical Christians have done very little to expose the false teachings of Hebrew Israelism.

Jude 3 exhorts Christians to "earnestly contend for the faith which was once delivered unto the saints". It is the church's responsibility to contend amongst and for all peoples, so the elect may be drawn to the Father amongst all peoples. Combatting false narratives should be written into every pastor's job description! In John 4, Jesus encounters Samaritan doctrinal idiosyncrasies ("which mountain is the right one to worship on?"). There is a parallel to be drawn between a group like the Samaritans of Israel and black and Hispanic Americans. As a despised minority in Israelite society, the Samaritan woman's objections were tied up in historical and cultural considerations (much like the doctrinal matrix of Hebrew Israelism).

Just as Jesus deftly answered the Samaritan woman's objections and confronted the false narrative she believed, Christians must "go and do thou likewise". In 1 Peter 3:15, the apostle commands Christians to be "prepared to make a defense to anyone who asks you for a reason for the hope that is in you". Different people in different contexts get asked different questions about the hope that is in them. A black Christian is more likely to hear these questions:

"Look at this picture of this white man. Why do you worship a white Jesus"?

"Don't you know your Bible is a history book of the black Israelites"?

"Why do you go to a church building, listen to a con man and pay him money"?

"Do you call the white man your brother and attend church with the Devil"?

Most white Christians do not face these objections. Yet, a "Hebrew Israelite" (and others like them) will ask these – and more. To reach the souls caught up in these groups, Christians must be prepared. Per Colossians 4:5-6, Christians need to be writing and speaking so that we may know how we ought to answer every man.

THE STORY BEHIND THIS BOOK

The "Hebrew Israelites" appeared on my radar a decade ago. One day, a friend from high school called. He told me about this group of men our age who were busting into churches around my old neighborhood on the south side of Columbus, Ohio. He says they would interrupt the service and begin yelling, disrupting everything, and then abruptly leave (years later, one of the camp leaders who led the "church storming" tactic told me they timed their exits to avoid the cops, who were often called by the parishioners). 7 My friend described their attire and behavior accurately; I successfully found their videos online at Live Leak. I discovered they called themselves "Great Mill Stone Israelites" (GMS). I watched every video I could find. It was wild to see them running around the Short North in the very spots I used to tag (I used to be a graffiti tagger, under the alias MAL ONE!).

One memorable video showed their leader, Aaron, and GMS Columbus preaching in Schiller Park. Schiller Park played a special part in my life. I played ball there. I broke a car window with a baseball there. I flirted with girls there. I hung out in the clubhouse there. My friends got jumped there. I first heard "Can't Touch This" in the parking lot there. One time, I even saw *Shakespeare in the Park* there. When I saw Aaron yelling at joggers telling them that what happened to Nicole Brown Simpson was just a preview of what was going to happen to all white women in the future, I was fascinated, shocked, and intrigued. I undertook a brief study on the movement. Then I forgot about it.[8]

Fast forward four years; I was living in Phoenix. I was on my way to the Arizona Collectors Market on 7th Ave. My mission that day was to buy an Incredible Hulk action figure for my son (at the time he was obsessed with the Green Goliath). On the way to the toy shop, I saw a group of "Hebrew Israelites" on the corner of 19th Ave. If I saw them on the way back to the crib, I decided I would engage. One hour and two Incredible Hulks later, they were still there, yelling at everybody exiting the Light Rail Train and cursing out anyone they perceived to be "effeminate", from "another nation", or in a "mixed relationship". Hitting record on my iPod, I strolled up and asked, "What is the gospel?" The loud and lively back and forth which ensued lasted over an hour. I went home and uploaded the lo-fi audio to my blog.[9] It blew up. It seemed as if everyone had a comment or question. It was as if people had been waiting years to talk about this but had no outlet. It felt like everyone had a story to share. I had no idea. People were coming to me as if I was an expert when I was just a student. I realized this was an underserved area and that people craved information and gospel answers. Very few people were interacting with this group from an apologetic or evangelistic perspective. Something needed to be done.

On August 2013, I spoke publicly on the "Hebrew Israelites" for the first time, on a radio program called Backpack Radio. My past apologetic endeavors were dominated by abortion, foster care and adoption advocacy, Mormons, Jehovah's Witnesses and the Nation of Islam. I was consumed with studying issues relating to Roman Catholicism, atheism, and especially Salafi Islam. I was swamped dealing with the apologetic issues I ran into on the Arizona State University campus and Mill Avenue.

My focus shifted in 2015, when I had to submit a proposal for my doctoral project at Talbot School of Theology in La Mirada, California. Even though the bulk of our instruction in the Doctorate of Ministry program dealt with graduate-level philosophy, I knew I wanted to do something less abstract, something more concrete, something more hands-on, something more practical, something more street-level. It came down to a project relating to witnessing at the masjid (mosque) after jimnah (Friday prayer at noon) or a project relating to Hebrew Israelism. After much prayer, discussion and contemplation, I submitted a proposal relating to Hebrew Israelism. My professors (JP Moreland and Garrett DeWeese) gave some revisions and then approved. Jeff, Luke, Marcus and Joy – my friends at Apologia TV – heard about all this and invited me to their studio in Tempe. My interview (they titled it "Black Hebrew Israelites Exposed") dropped May 2016. In July 2016, I did three programs on Hebrew Israelism on Dr. James White's "Dividing Line". These events were a catalyst.

Since then, a lot has happened on this front. Phone calls, Google hangouts, radio interviews, Periscope broadcasts, Facebook groups, tweets, debates, response videos, conferences, face to face sit downs and more real life street encounters. Some great new websites have been published recently (UrbanApologetics.Org and dahorton.org). A few counter-apologetic debate crews have been established: Narrow Way Apologetics, Black Urban Apologetics, Soldiers of God, and The Shield Squad (of which I am a member).[10] RAAN (Reformed African-American Network) has published good articles, but by far, the Jude3 Project is the most multi-faceted, large-scale, and successful venture in the area of urban apologetics (shout out to Lisa Fields and Cam Triggs). And now here I am, hoping to contribute my five loaves and two fishes, writing this booklet. *#onward*

CHAPTER 1 ENDNOTES

1.https://www.viceland.com/en_us/show/hate-thy-neighbor. Accessed 01/24/2017.

2. This clip is online: https://www.youtube.com/watch?v=BJUD4c5ba5w. Accessed 9/6/17.

3. & 4. For the message board thread, I have screenshots on file. Listen to "Unequally Yoked: Victims of 1West Relations". This aired on Debate Talk 4U (4/17).

5. Here are several helpful articles and perspectives on this phenomenon (please note: links do not equal endorsement): "America's Changing Landscape".http://www.pewforum.org/2015/05/12/americas-changing-religious-landscape. "Are Men Missing From the Black Church?". http://www.naltblackchurch.com/blackmen-missing.html. "The Black Church is Dead". http://www.huffingtonpost.com/eddie-glaude-jr-phd/the-black-church-is-dead_b_473815.html. "Are Black Millenials Being Pushed Out of the Church?". https://www.washingtonpost.com/blogs/local/wp/2013/08/27/are-black-millennials-being-pushed-out-of-the-church/?utm_term=.6f3d7ef15d87. "Why Are Young Blacks Leaving the Church?". https://9marks.org/article/why-are-young-blacks-leaving-the-church. I also found articles relaying the challenge gentrification presents to the church in four key areas: Washington, DC; Seattle, WA; Oakland, CA, and Harlem, NY. All accessed 1/28/2017.

6. The most prominent is an entry at Christian Apologetics Research Ministry: https://carm.org/black-hebrew-israelites. Accessed 01/24/2017. Matt Slick (CARM Founder) said it is one of their most accessed articles. https://soundcloud.com/biblethumpingwingnut/btwn-episode-189. Accessed 01/24/2017.

7. 2 Corinthians 11:4

8. Some Hebrew Israelites have accused me of lying about the church storming incidents to make their movement look bad. The leader of the aforementioned crew is named Rex Scientia (Aaron). He has publicly confirmed my account. In the YouTube video, "A Shout Out to Vocab Malone My Fellow Southsider Lolz", Rex recollects: "We made a series of videos called 'Church Hunters' and we would just run up in churches and curse everybody out ... we tried to give them the truth and they rejected us. Then we cursed them out and then they called the cops and then we dipped". Accessed 6/10/17.

9. In Summer 2017, I visited this same camp twice. We debated and I tried to share the gospel with those who stopped by. For one example, see "PT3 Vocab Malone Stops by the Camp". https://www.youtube.com/watch?v=tZMg-fn4u30. Accessed 08/16/2017.

10. I uploaded the audio in December 2011. I believe the encounter with GMS Phoenix took place November 2011.

11. We introduced our urban apologetics crew to the public a few times, such as here: https://theshieldsquad.wordpress.com/2017/06/15/introducing-the-shield-squad and here http://www.blogtalkradio.com/debatetalk4u/2017/08/02/the-hot-seat-wshield-squad-meet-the-new-recruits. Both accessed 9/6/17.

"The Human Antecedents of the residents of Harlem, USA were Hebrews in Spain, in Egypt and in Ethiopia; the ancient Hebrew-Israelites have millions of descendants in HARLEM, USA ... and 'Harlem's' elsewhere."

– Hebrew Israelite author Lacy G. Blair in *Harlem's Hebrew Israelites.*

WHAT IS 1WEST? BASIC BELIEFS

Barack Obama is not originally from the South Side of Chicago, but it is the spot where he sprouted, politically speaking. Thinking of him representing Chicago's South Side is an interesting exercise as we look at the debate scene in *Barry*. The modern landscape of US Hebrew Israelism has significant streams flowing out of these two metro areas: Harlem, New York and the South Side of Chicago. Imagining Obama's mini-debate as symbolic of the two strands, some of their differences are demarcated. Let me demonstrate with a slice of the dialogue (this interaction is between an intoxicated white female in the crowd and the "Hebrew Israelite" speaker):

> **HEBREW ISRAELITE:** Can the prey be taken from the mighty or the captives of a tyrant rescued? Now what that means is (referring to Isaiah 49:24), can we, as the Lost Tribe of Israel, reclaim what is rightfully ours from the cave-dwelling white devils that raped our ancestors, stole our land and dispersed the true children of God[1] across the globe? READ!

DRUNK WOMAN: *(slurred)* Hey! I ain't ... no ... devil! This is not the words of Jesus Christ.

HEBREW ISRAELITE: Shut your mouth, cave b****!

DRUNK WOMAN: *(taken aback, with a look of shocked surprise)*

HEBREW ISRAELITE: Yes, you are a cave b****. Do you know what Jesus Christ called the white woman in the Bible? A female dog. And what is a female dog?

CAMERA PANS TO CROWD, SPEAKER POINTS TO AUDIENCE MEMBER

HEBREW ISRAELITE: Don't be afraid to say it, brother. That's right, a b****. That's what Jesus Christ called you in the Bible.

Here is one big difference between the Harlem-originated 1Westers and the Chicago-originated "Hebrew Israelites": an Israel of God member would never call a white woman walking a "cave b****". In fact, they probably wouldn't even be out street teaching. This does not mean they are small. On the contrary, Israel of God's Chicago building holds 6,000 people. No other "Hebrew Israelite" group I know of has a building that size.[2] There are a number of "Hebrew Israelite" groups associated with Chicago: Israel of God, the African Hebrew Israelites of Jerusalem[3] and Beth Shalom B'nai Zaken Ethiopian Hebrew Congregation.[4]

"Hebrew Israelite" groups out of 1West in Harlem (save GOCC) do not believe "other nations" can be grafted into Israel proper. In short, they can only be enemies – never brothers. Israel of God is different. Their theology still includes ethnic hierarchy – they call it "the protocol" – but it is a softer and gentler ethnic hierarchy. Brother Henry Buie is the head pastor of Israel of God. In the notes for his lesson titled, "Black

History as Told by the Prophets, Part 1 – Color", he wrote this on Acts 10: "God brought Gentiles (which Israelites looked at as common and unclean) into the church. This chapter isn't saying you can eat anything you want, it's talking about bringing non-Israelites into the body of Christ (the church/commonwealth of Israel)".[5] A Seventh Day Adventist exegete would basically interpret this passage the same way.

IOG and GOCC believe "Gentiles" can be grafted in but 1Westers do not think Gentiles can even be "saved". They believe that neither the law nor salvation was given for any other nation except Israel. "What you heathens don't realize is", states a member of the GMS Las Vegas Camp, "you don't understand that the Good News is only for us. The reason why ... it's not considered the gospel for you is because the good message is not for you, it's not towards you – you have no part in that. That's why you don't believe that that's the Good News or the gospel".

In the same video ("Vocab Malone: We Will Be Kicking the Heathen A** in the Kingdom According to the Gospel"), the GMS Vegas member asks a rhetorical question: "Who's promised salvation? Only the nation of Israel". At one point, a GMS Vegas member further defines the gospel this way: Ezekiel 25:14 "means we're going to be beating ya'll a**, we going be f*****g you up. We're going to take vengeance on you". According to the GMS Vegas member, here's part of what that means: "All of the other nations, we're going to take their riches. We're going to take their women." Then it gets personal: "You got that Vocab Malone? ... If you're an Israelite, you're going to be whipping the heathen's a** too in the Kingdom. You don't even realize that, man. The Lord's going to have you whipping a** in the kingdom - if it turns out that you're one of us". Should I be flattered?[6]

IT DON'T MATTER IF YOU'RE BLACK OR WHITE

A twist to their exclusivist teaching is that a few camps, including GMS, teach that since Israel was so scattered, modern "Hebrew Israelites" could "appear" to be white! So even though GMS teaches no so-called white man can be saved (their language), if you click on any video featuring GMS Columbus or search for "GMS white" on YouTube, you will see some GMS spokesmen who look Caucasian. You will also see other "Hebrew Israelite" camps criticizing GMS for this policy. Here's the irony: GMS, often considered the most bigoted, foul-mouthed and verbally abusive camp around, allows "white looking Hebrew Israelites" to teach and even lead local chapters. Yet, Israel of God, the most moderate "camp" (they function somewhat like a small denomination), will not allow any perceived "non-Israelite", be they Asian, Arabian or Indian to teach over perceived "Israelites" (read: black folks). Israel of God claims this would be "out of order".

I have personally attended an Israel of God meeting in Phoenix. I brought two friends: one black, one white. The congregants treated both friends with equal respect. They heard us out and they let us speak. One man offered me his seat. Another offered me his lunch. A man named Jedidah took my address and number (he has been very generous in sending study materials. We still speak kindly on the phone; he invites me to special events). I respect the members from Israel of God Phoenix.[7] We should recognize the differences between Israel of God and the 1Westers. Yet, these warm remarks are not to be misconstrued as an endorsement of their theology. Granted, Israel of God has fewer problems than any given 1West camp, but they still have some problems. The biggest problem with IoG is their doctrine of the Holy Spirit. This, from their website:

> *The Holy Spirit is not the third part of the "Trinity". There are currently only two members in the Godhead, The Father and His Son, Jesus Christ. The Holy Spirit can be manifested to man*

> *in many forms. One form is an Angel sent from God to bring to remembrance what Jesus has told us in His Holy Word (another form of His Spirit). The Word that the Angel brings to man is the power, thoughts, and spiritual extension of God. God begets true Christians as His sons and daughters through this Spirit (God's Word). It strengthens a Christian spiritually, converts his mind, and serves as an earnest, or beginning, of the transformation to obtain eternal life.*[8]

Any Christian should be able to spot the problems in Israel of God's pneumatology. If not, it's time to get on that 2 Timothy 2:15: "Study to shew thyself approved unto God, a workman that needeth not to be ashamed, rightly dividing the word of truth".[9] I debated an Israel of God member Brother Alvin on the personhood and deity of the Holy Spirit on a "Hebrew Israelite" debate platform, Debate Talk 4U. We also discussed their claims of "proper protocols" for people they see as "Gentiles". Overall, it was a very enlightening and yet somewhat disheartening discussion.[10]

Back to the *Barry* movie: in the debate scene, young Obama challenges the "Hebrew Israelite" speaker after he witnesses him verbally beat up an intoxicated white woman. This is Chicago vs. Harlem. The "Hebrew Israelites" who trace their theological roots back to 1West at Harlem are the ones some readers may have seen on their local city block. 1West styled "Hebrew Israelism" appears to be ascending, growing in numbers, influence, presence and volume. It all started in 1969. What follows is a *small* part of the story.

As you hopefully understand by now, there are many religious groups who in some way identify as "Hebrew Israelites". The most visible, by way of street corners and YouTube videos, are the main subject of this booklet. Below is a brief list. Some of the "Hebrew Israelite" groups which can be classified as 1Westers are listed on the next page:

NOTE: *Both of the following charts are partial and incomplete listings. I add camps and details as I discover them. For an online (and hopefully updated) list, visit:* https://theshieldsquad.wordpress.com/hebrew-israelite-camps-list/

1WEST (MESSIANIC, HARLEM-SCHOOL INFLUENCED) CAMPS
Ambassadors of Christ (AOC) – New York
Brothers United in Christ – defunct/inactive - ?
Future World of Israel (FWOI) - Virginia
Gathering of Christ Church (GOCC) – New York
Great MillStone Israelites (GMS) - Connecticut
House of David – (HOD) – Brooklyn, New York
House of Israel – defunct/inactive (HOI) - New York
Israel United in Christ (IUIC) – New York
Israelite Church of God in Jesus Christ (ICGJC) http://www.icgjcmd.org/ - New Jersey
Israelite School of Biblical History & Practical Knowledge (ISBPK) - Texas
Israelite School of Knowledge (ISOK) - Virginia
Israelite School of Universal Practical Knowledge (ISUPK) - Harlem, NY
Lions of Israel / We Got Next (LOI) - Brooklyn, NY
OneBody In Yahawashi - Dallas, TX
Saints of Thunder (fka Sons of Thunder) – Brooklyn, NY
Shield of Wisdom – Los Angeles, CA
Shut 'Em Down Crew / RAM Squad (Internet Debate Crew) - Florida
Sicarii – San Diego, CA
The Light and Body Church – defunct/inactive
Thee Light of Zion
Tribe of Judah – Dallas, TX
True Nation Israelite Congregation - http://truenation.org/
Yahawashi's Servants in Y'Sharael – Phoenix, AZ
14th Street Israelites – New York

NOTE: *The groups listed below follow Hebrew Israelism in a variety of manners. They are "Hebrew Israelites" in some way but they are not ideological descendants of 1West.*

NON-1WEST "HEBREW ISRAELITES"
TANAKH-Only Camps / Congregations / Synagogue
African Hebrew Israelites of Jerusalem
1Beit DCB - www.shmayisrael.com/Truth/TheTrueHouseofIsrael.html
Church of God and Saints of Christ (est. by William Saunders Crowdy)
Commandment Keepers
Torah Knights (Internet Debate Crew)
Messianic / Hebrew Roots & "Hebrew Israelite" Mixture
Absolute Bible Truth (Internet Debate Group)
Church of the Living God, the Pillar Ground of Truth for All Nations (est. by F.S. Cherry)
Destined Ministries – Stephen Darby (Louisville, KY)
Huldah Daiu - www.herroyalroots.com
Kingdom Harbinger Ministries (Ron "Divine Prospect" Shields) – Atlanta, GA ***NOTE:*** *the KHM group and its teacher dub themselves RBG Brews. RBG refers to the African colors of Red, Black and Green. The idea is to combine Hebrew Israelism, elements of the Conscious Community, Pan-Africanism and some mainstream secular scholarship.*
Nation of Yahweh – Miami, FL
School of the Hebrews at Philadelphia Christian Church - Omar Thibeaux (Lafeyette, LA)
Straitway Truth (Pastor Dowell) – Tennessee
Torah to the Tribes – Matthew Moshe Nolan (Salem, Oregon)
The Way of Yah Synagogue of Yahushah - www.thewayofyah.com (Pastor Tony Smith)
Chicago-Influenced Messianic
The Israel of God – Chicago, IL
Congregation of Israel, Knesset of Jesus (of The Nazarene Messianic Party) – Buffalo, NY

ADVENTURES IN PIONEERING AN ABERRANT SECT

NOTE: *for this next section I am indebted to Abu Khamr, founder of Truth after Knowledge. He allowed me to revise an article he wrote years ago. I would not be able to write the history section if it was not for his work and generosity.*

The ideological descendants classified as 1Westers all have their beginnings in a religious school that was headquartered at 1 West 125th Street in Harlem. The school began in 1969. It was originally called the Israelite School of Torah and located on 5th Avenue in Harlem. The school was run by a man named Abba Bivens (later, it would be led by a group of leaders called "The Seven Heads"). It is said that Bivens was first told he was an "Israelite" by an ex-slave in the South. Bivens relocated to New York and joined the Commandment Keepers under Chief Rabbi Wentworth Arthur Matthews.[11]

Eventually, Bivens rejected the Old Testament only teaching and broke away from the Black Jewish congregation. In 1969, Bivens began the aforementioned Israelite School of Torah (he was later considered to be John the Baptist reincarnate by his followers). It is said that the ceremonial practices of the school originated from the late Elder Yaiqab (Peter Sherrod), who is rumored to have acquired these teachings from the late Abba Bivens and the late W.A. Matthew in the 1960s.[12]

Bivens was murdered by some Muslim men he debated in Newark, New Jersey. Three of his students, Arieh, Mosheh, and Yakob (Ahrayah's father) began a new school, right around the corner at 1 West 125th Street in Harlem. They changed the name to the Israelite School of Universal Practical Knowledge. Arieh, introduced a number of significant innovations: belief in the King James Bible, the 12 Tribes Chart and his own version of Hebrew ("Lashawan Qadash"). He later introduced the failed year 2000 prophecy (he predicted Christ would return in 2000). Arayah based this "prophecy" off of Hosea 6.[13]

The change in spelling Arayah's name (Arieh to Arayah) requires an explanation. The reason is "Harlem Hebrew". This esoteric "language" of 1West requires an excursus.

A-E-I-O-U AND SOMETIMES ONLY A

Lashawan qadash ("holy tongue") is Modern Israeli Hebrew with all the vowels except 'a' taken out. He also introduced the claim that the *ayin* can only be pronounced like the 'i' in pie.[14] Proponents of Lashawan Qadash don't usually know Hebrew, they often just memorize various Hebrew words and purposefully mispronounce them (e.g., "shalawam" instead of "shalom," or "Yahawashi" instead of "Y'hoshu`a"). 1Westers assert actual Hebrew is mere "Yiddish" and that their version of Hebrew is the only true form. With the introduction of Lashawan Qadash, Arieh changed his name to Ahrayah. His associate Elder Moshe Ben Chareem became Mashah.

REINCARNATION KEEPS COMING BACK

The name changed to the Israeli Church of Universal Practical Knowledge (some speculate this was for tax exemption status). In the mid-90s, there was a split in the ICUPK between Ahrayah and Mashah (fka Elder Moshe Ben Chareem). Ahrayah was leader of the school but made the mistake of teaching Mashah was King David reincarnated.[15] Thus, when Mashah left, members who thought he was the reincarnation of King David left with him. Mashah's new group began meeting at 126th St. and was called, alternatively, the House of David (or 12Tribes). When Mashah died in 1999, the House of David group split into several groups. One remnant of the group still calls itself the House of David.[16] Another breakaway group from House of David called itself the House of Israel.[17]

THE STRAW THAT BROKE ARAYAH'S BACK

To recap: all those groups were splinters from the House of David group which left the ICUPK, and then broke apart after Mashah, their leader, died. Meanwhile, the ICUPK suffered a terrible set back when Ahrayah predicted and declared frequently and confidently that Christ would come back to kill or enslave all "non-Israelites" on January 1st, 2000. When the time came and went without fulfillment, there was a crisis of faith in the ICUPK. A low-ranking member named Tazadaqyah (Jermaine Grant) rose to power even over Ahrayah (allegedly via intimidation). The ICUPK changed their name to the Israelite Church of God in Jesus Christ (ICGJC). Tazadaqyah's titles are expansive: Apostle and Chief High Priest Tazadaqyah, also known as the Comforter (opponents dubbed him "Comfy"). While visiting Israel, it is said Tazadaqyah had a revelation and was henceforth declared to be "the Comforter", i.e., the Holy Spirit in the form of a man.[18]

THE FRACTURED 21ST CENTURY

These groups, though slowly developing doctrines different from one another, all agree that true Jews are "melinated peoples", and that Genesis 25:25 proves that "Edomites" are white (they claim white people are actually red, as their blood shows through their face due to a lack of melanin). It has been noted many times that the Hebrew word used in Genesis 25:25 to describe Esau as "red" is also used to describe David in 1 Samuel 16:12. They ignore the Hebrew text and say a different word is used because their King James Bible has "ruddy" (which they claim means young!) in 1 Samuel 16:12. Most "Hebrew Israelites" are KJV-Onlyists or something close to that position. Additionally, 1Westers hold the Apocrypha as canonical. Some 1West groups claim they are the only ones with the truth, such as ICGJC and especially the ISUPK. Many groups mutually hate one another. There have been a few infamous street brawls. One notorious incident took place between GMS and ICGJC.

DON'T WRITE CHECKS...

Historically, 1Westers have claimed no one can stand in debate with them and that the world's scholars are afraid of them. This changed in 2016, when Dr. James White debated Elder Rachaar of GOCC and handily defeated him twice. It wasn't just that Dr. White clearly won; it was that the Elder made himself look as if he did not understand proper argumentation, what constitutes evidence for a claim and the concept of primary sources. For example, at one point during the debate when James White asked Rachaar for a primary source for a claim, Rachaar cited a book called *Illuminati II* by Henry Makow.[19] Needless to say, the book is *not* a primary source, unless a scholar was defending a thesis titled "The Convergence of Anti-Semitism and Conspiracy Theories in Modern America".

The reality was exposed: 1West doctrine is weak. Frequently, when confronted with arguments they can't handle, 1Westers resort to personal attacks ("look at that demon coming off of him", "he's got a sodomite spirit", "he's the damn devil the Bible speaks of", "he hates black people and has a racist agenda", or "he's a little niglet coon"). They will assert that others who disagree with them do so because God has blinded them while they themselves get their truth "straight from the Most High". Ironically, many 1West offshoots keep changing their doctrines.

A recent example is when IUIC began changing the way they calculate the New Moon (which is important for when they keep the feasts). IUIC went from teaching that the Full Moon is not the New Moon on 2013,[20] to teaching that the Full Moon is the New Moon on 2016.[21] Here we see the 1West pendulum swing: they claim to be the only ones with the truth when they taught one thing and continue to claim to be the only ones with the truth when they teach the exact opposite. This is why my friend Cadaash (an ex-member) quips, "The only thing 1Westers are consistent in is in being inconsistent". In short, they are consistently inconsistent.

WHAT WE'RE GONNA DO RIGHT HERE IS GO BACK, WAY BACK

Even though this wave of "Hebrew Israelites" traces back its ideological roots to 1969 at 1 West in Harlem, they were not the first Black Americans to claim to be ethnic "Israelites". All "Hebrew Israelites" believe there is an inevitable awakening happening as individuals come to the knowledge about their true heritage as God's chosen people. Some believe the first eyelid began cracking open in 1896. "Hebrew Israelite" author Ella Hughley writes that "The prophecy of Ezekiel chapter 37 and many others began their modern-day fulfillment in 1896" ... "when a prophet of the Almighty God, William Saunders Crowdy, resurrected and re-established the house of Israel in Lawrence, Kansas."[22] It's true Crowdy was one of the first people to clearly expound this idea in a serious way. What exactly happened with Crowdy (1847-1908) in 1896? According to the Church of God and Saints of Christ (the church he officially founded in November 8, 1896) website, this is the account:

> *One day while felling trees, the hand and the Spirit of the Lord were heavy upon him. ... He heard a voice telling him to run for his life. He became disturbed, and fled into the woods, thinking that he was going to die. ...*
>
> *It was during his sojourn in the wild that the Almighty God revealed to Prophet William S. Crowdy the "Ancient Plan of Salvation" as taught by Moses and the other biblical prophets.*
>
> *... Those same truths which the former prophets had fostered were heralded again by this Prophet of God: the Sabbath (Saturday), the Passover, the Hebrew Calendar, the Day of Atonement, and above all, the Ten Commandments of the Sinai Revelation.*
>
> *As he strove to re-establish this doctrine and gather the lost sheep of the House of Israel (Matthew 10:6), he met with much*

> *opposition from some of his listeners and from some of the civil authorities. While preaching on the streets, he was arrested 22 times, however, he continued the mission on which he had been sent.*[23]

Hughley and others like her believe the work of awakening Israelites to their true heritage began in 1896 with Crowdy and continues to this day. There is debate about whether the modern camps are truly continuing the same trajectory began by Crowdy. Although the post-60s groups (especially IUIC) link what they do with Crowdy, it is not a true straight line from dot to dot. Crowdy was not as radical as many of the modern groups and even had black and white followers.

One informed commentator, Sar-Sharaht Ma'asehyahu, believes Crowdy would be appalled by these attempts to link him with the current manifestation of Hebrew Israelism. A visit to the IUIC website shows they are clearly trying to link themselves to Crowdy's work but some people who identify as Hebrew Israelites disagree strongly: "I noticed in the last two years, that they have now been creating charts in which they trace themselves back to Crowdy", observes Sar-Sharaht Ma'asehyahu, "Crowdy's group disavows everything that they're about because Crowdy's first followers - as an ex-slave who maintained this tradition – his first followers were actually white. So he's diametrically opposed to everything they stand for".[24]

Another early movement within Hebrew Israelism includes Warren Roberson who founded the Temple of The Gospel of The Kingdom in Virginia in 1900. In 1917, Roberson moved the headquarters to Harlem. In 1917, F.S. Cherry established the Church of God in Philadelphia. It is said Cherry's doctrine was influenced by both Crowdy and Roberson. In 1919, Wentworth Matthews founded the Commandments Keepers in Harlem. In 1930, Arnold Josiah Ford established the Beth B'nai Abraham congregation and this was incorporated into the Commandment Keepers congregation. *#nextchapter #moreheresy*

CHAPTER 2 ENDNOTES

1. There is an imprecision in the dialogue. The main speaker is clearly a 1Wester from the original school at 1West 125th St. in Harlem and yet he is not using the sect's version of Hebrew called "Lashawan Qadash". What he would have said for God is YAHAWAH. For Jesus, he would have said YAHAWASHI. I imagine the writer did not want these words to get lost in (mis)translation.

2. See the Chicago CBS local online article, "Riverdale Mayor Hardly Excited About Church Replacing Vacant Lot", June 25, 2012 by Dorothy Tucker. Additionally, in one talk, Israel of God leader Pastor Henry Buie, humble brags about the denomination's size. The video is titled, "Israel of God is the Biggest Hebrew Israelite Congregation in the World".

3. There is a "Hebrew Israelite" community in Dimona, Israel (estimates number 4-5,000). The AHIOJ have been written on extensively: *The Heritage Seekers: Black Jews in Search of Identity* by Israel J. Gerber (1977) and *Thin Description: Ethnography and the African Hebrew Israelites of Jerusalem* by John L. Jackson, Jr. (2013).

4. Even though Gathering of Christ Church (GOCC) falls under the 1West umbrella, their leader, Elder Rachaar has been partially influenced by Chicago-style Hebrew Israelism.

5. http://www.theisraelofgod.com/wp-content/uploads/2017/02/2-04-17-BlackHistory-Pt1-Color-BW1.pdf. Accessed 6/11/17.

6. https://www.youtube.com/watch?v=sxD6MWROJ8c. Accessed 9/6/17.

7. Even though I have warm feelings towards many Israel of God members, they still have members who can become relatively contentious when they feel their doctrine is being challenged. Witness the slew of attack videos by Chicago IOG stalwart Mikha'el Ben Yisreal.

8. http://www.israelofgodatl.com/iog-atl--about.html. Accessed 6/11/17. Here are the Scripture references the website gives for the pneumatology section: Genesis 1:2; Exodus 23:20; Judges 2:1-4; Isaiah 63:9; Romans 12:1-2; Psalm 104:4; John 14:26; 15:26; 16:13-15; Acts 7:52-53; Hebrews 1:13-14; Revelation 1:1-2; 22:6, 16.

9. I recommend D.A. Horton's *DNA: Foundations of the Faith for an intro to systematic theology* and Dr. Richard A. Robinson's *God, Torah and Messiah: The Messianic Theology of Dr. Louis Goldberg* for a more expansive systematic theology, including sections on the person and work of the Holy Spirit. A helpful book from the charismatic perspective is Gordon D. Fee's *Paul, the Spirit, and the People of God*.

10. http://www.blogtalkradio.com/debatetalk4u/2017/06/01/similarities-differences-dialogue-wvocab-malone-brother-alvin. Accessed 6/11/17.

11. There are many books on this congregation: *The Black Jews of Harlem: Negro Nationalism and the Dilemmas of Negro Leadership* by Howard M. Brotz (1964); *Black Jews in America: A Documentary with Commentary* by Graenum Berger (1978); *Judaising Movements: Studies in the Margins of Judaism* by Tudor Parfitt and EmanuelaTrevisan Semi (2002).

12. This is according to the current House of David website, http://hodc12.webs.com/ahic.htm. Accessed 8/28/17.

13. To see a compilation of various speakers predicting this, watch the YouTube video "Black Hebrew Israelites False Year 2000 Prophecy".

14. To hear an explanation and critical analysis of what I have dubbed "Harlem Hebrew", watch the "Lashawan Qadash Takedown" video https://www.youtube.com/watch?v=mXZJqYfyO5M. Accessed 8/28/2017.

15. A key figure named Wahab left the school in 1999 over the King David teaching. Most 1West Hebrew Israelites hold to reincarnation, which they call "regeneration".

16. Their YouTube account is at *hodc12*, standing for House of David Church 12 Tribes.

17. Their YouTube videos can be seen at *thehouseofisrael*.

18. Apparently, Comfy has competition: another "Israelite" is calling himself the Holy Ghost: http://kingyahwehtheholyghost.com. Accessed 9/6/17.

19. I had a remarkably similar experience with Judah Nazareth, a TANKH-Only "Hebrew Israelite". During a video debate, he kept asserting Jesus was a rip-off from Osiris. I asked him to provide one primary source for his claim. He eventually agreed to my request and proceeded to pull out a book called "the Encyclopedia of Freemasonry". Remember, this was his answer to the question, "what is a primary source that supports the claim that Jesus was actually Osiris remixed. Watch this exchange titled "Vocab Malone Gets Destroyed Again" at https://www.youtube.com/watch?v=ccuJBHd9sfQ&t=405s. Accessed 8/28/17.

20. "New Moon Feast IUIC", https://www.youtube.com/watch?v=7aocdAJbef0. Accessed 6/11/17.

21. "The Israelites: Full Moon is the New Moon", https://www.youtube.com/watch?v=k3ovFkL7x78. Accessed 6/11/17.

22. Ella J. Hughley, *The Truth About Black Biblical Hebrew-Israelites* (Springfield Gardens, NY: Hughley Productions, 1982), 29.

23. http://www.cogasoc.org/leaders/wscrowdy.html. Accessed 8/4/16.

24. Hear his comments at 1:20:00: http://thelineoffire.org/2017/02/02/focus-on-the-usa-and-israel-then-on-black-hebrew-israelites. Accessed 6/12/17.

*"No African, no Asian, no Chinese, no white man, no German, no Russian, no Caucasian, no non-Israelite will ever eat with me at anything that ISUPK is having or I'm having, period. ... ya'll can take that blackitty-black s*** around the corner. Non-Israelites will not come to the cookout, period. ... the scripture say "prepare slaughter for his children for the iniquity of the fathers". So because of the crimes that the forefathers committed against us is why I want them white babies to die."*

– Captain Tazaryach of the ISUPK[1]

WHAT IS 1WEST? BASIC BELIEFS

In *Barry*, PJ is one of Obama's friends. Many reviewers believe that PJ represents the common black experience in the United States. While PJ keeps Obama "grounded", they don't seem to fully understand each other. A 1Wester might say that is because the two have a "different spirit". According to 1West Hebrew Israelism, although PJ is called a black man, he is actually an "Israelite". But PJ is not "woke" to his true heritage; he is a "Jake" who is in a "deep sleep". "Jake" is short for Jacob, which was Israel's name prior to his wrestling match with an angel (Genesis 32:24-30).

Jason Mitchell, who played PJ in *Barry*, is a perfect example of a "Jake" (per the 1West understanding). His best known acting role was Eazy-E in *Straight Outta Compton*. Mitchell also played a drug smuggler in the 2012 movie, *Contraband*. This means he's portrayed a rapper and a criminal. 1Westers see this as standard "pre-Israelite awareness" or "Jake" behavior. 1Westers regularly say prejudiced and bigoted things towards the community. Stereotypes 1Westers commonly pass on about

"Jakes" are they are addicted to church (1Westers believe this often gives Jakes a spirit of Sodomy), effeminate, or coons who just want a hug of affirmation from "Esau", the so-called white man.

If black people in the US are "asleep" and need to be awakened to their true identity, how can this be accomplished? The 1West answer is street teaching, going into the highways and byways. And what exactly do they teach? That's what this chapter is about.

EZEKIEL 37 OR NAH?

Partially because the leaders are aware of the movement's growth and partially because many of them believe the "time of the Gentiles" (the time of "white" domination) must end 400-430 years after the beginning of slaves coming to the shores of what would become the United States of America[2], "Hebrew Israelites" generally believe they are living in a time of prophetic fulfillment, the time when the valley of dry bones comes to life.[3] After of bevy of comments where a leader of IUIC was responding to criticism by Christian apologists, he punctuated his statements with this admonition: "This is not a game – you're living Bible prophecy, you're living it". Here is the aforementioned bevy:

> *This movement is set up to destroy their world. Ya'll don't understand this. This whole thing is a room full of men who plan to destroy this society's doctrines – everything. Once we are successful in our mission, this world ends. They're not going to allow you to do that without a fight. Wouldn't you fight back? I would. Unless you're scared but Esau's not scared. Within 200 plus years he done conquered the whole world – America is a fresh, a new country – this isn't old. America was established in so-called 1776 and conquered everybody within a matter of time. All thanks to their god, the devil. But that's what they did. So they're not going to just hand the world over to what they call a bunch of n***** and spics and savages – they're not*

doing that. They're not going to sit by idle and allow you to get organized amongst yourselves either. So be mindful.[4]

IS THIS THE AWAKENING OF THE DRY BONES?

"Some people have believed for many years," well known "Hebrew Israelite" author Windsor explains, "the 'dry bones' refers to the resurrection of billions of dead people at the time of the coming of the Messiah. They couldn't be further from the truth. When we study the complete Bible, and all the book of Ezekiel, we see that there is clear proof the 'dry bone' refer only to an ancient race and their sons, and they do not refer to the actual dead in their graves".[5]

Windsor elaborates, claiming "the valley is America" and the bodies Ezekiel saw were dead "and the black man in America has no life".[6] Two pages and thirteen reasons later, Windsor summarizes: "We have learned that the bones, sinews, and flesh represent the unification of dispersed families after the emancipation from slavery and the skin represents the attaining of higher positions in all areas of American life, with the assistance of the federal laws".[7] This is how Windsor interprets Ezekiel 37. What about the question of the breath? Windsor says it represents many things, including "black nationalism":

> *... the law and spirit of God, a return to the African-Hebrew-Israelite-Judean identity, nationality, culture, history, and language. It is the acquisition of tremendous racial pride; it is the removal of the decadent slave mentality. It is black nationalism, is the utilization of this African-Hebrew-Israelite culture to acquire stupendous economical power to help solve the increasing unemployment problem. This breath will revitalize the black man, bring him to life, and impart to him knowledge and the understanding to direct his affairs in every compartment of life so that the masses of black communities will be safe from destroying themselves.*[8]

Can it be demonstrated this is what Ezekiel 37 is about? Most commentators agree this passage is at least about the recreation of Israel through divine power.[9] Prior to this, God's people have been justly judged. Exiled in Babylon, Israel is hopeless, helpless and lifeless. Yet, through the power of God's *ruach*, they may experience new life (37:9). The prophet is called to proclaim this truth.

Here is the question: what does it mean to re-create Israel? Some people believe this anticipates the present political state of Israel. "Hebrew Israelites" disagree, of course. Both the dispensationalist and the "Hebrew Israelite" interpretation miss the importance of this prophecy: Jesus Christ, as the New Israel, fulfills this passage by his resurrection.

Commentator Iain Duguid notes that the connections back to Ezekiel 36:24–38 make it clear "something more than political autonomy for the descendants of Abraham. It is nothing short of the fulfillment of all Old Testament anticipations of eschatological fullness, all of which are fulfilled in Christ. It is in him that the new Spirit-filled Israel of God takes shape, an identity that is no longer governed by ethnic origins and circumcision, as the old Israel was, but rather by faith in the cross of Christ (Gal. 6:12–16)."[10] Christopher Wright points out that the breath that gave the dead life came from the four winds, for "the Spirit of God is at work everywhere in the world, in all directions."[11] Christ himself echoes Ezekiel 37 in John 20:22, when he breathes on his disciples and tells them, "Receive the Holy Spirit."

Lastly, with the Genesis 2 imagery (breath/wind/spirit *ruach* in 37:9, 14) found in Ezekiel 37, there is a link between Israel and all of humanity. Abraham was called to be a blessing to all nations and Israel's election was for the redemption of all kinds of people, for "resurrection for Israel anticipated resurrection for all."[12]

TEN BELIEFS OF 1WEST HEBREW ISRAELISM
1West "Hebrew Israelites" believe that blacks, Hispanics, and Native Americans living in the Western Hemisphere whose ancestors were oppressed are the true descendants of Biblical Israel.
1West "Hebrew Israelites" believe that modern day Jews are fake impostors and not truly descendants of Jacob.
1West "Hebrew Israelites" usually hold the King James Version as authoritative. Very few 1Westers are "Tanakh-Only" but almost all believe the Apocrypha is canonical.
1West "Hebrew Israelites" believe the US and its allies will soon be judged because "Edomites" (white people) rule the earth and "Esau" (white people) marks the end of "the time of the Gentiles."
1West "Hebrew Israelites" believe salvation is procured by law-keeping. Sabbath-observance, dietary restrictions, and a certain outward appearance (beards and fringes)are marks of spiritual understanding and holiness.
1West "Hebrew Israelites" believe Jesus Christ was a black man with "negroid features" (their words).
Almost all 1West "Hebrew Israelites" believe people of "other nations" (Europeans, Arabs, Asians, Indians) cannot be saved. "Gentiles" are destined for either death or eternal servitude (via reincarnation) to "Israelites" in the Kingdom. A small minority believes "non-Hebrew Israelites" can be grafted into the Kingdom if they submit to a "Hebrew Israelite" and keep the law.
1West "Hebrew Israelites" believe both heaven and hell are merely "states of mind" or conditions. Neither are metaphysical realities as they are in orthodox Christianity.
1West "Hebrew Israelites" teach that Yahweh's name is either "Yahuah" or "Ahayah" and that Yeshua's name is either "Yahawashi" or "Yashayah."
1West "Hebrew Israelites" believe their duty is to gather scattered "Israelites" who are still "Jakes" – those who do not yet know the alleged truth of their ancestry and heritage.

ELAMITES & EDOMITES: FRATRENIZING WITH OTHER NATIONS

At Colombia, Barack Obama's roommate at East 94th Street was a Pakistani named Sohale Siddiqi ("Saleem" in *Barry*). For a 1Wester, this is a problem: fraternizing with other nations. Indians and Pakistanis are not included on the standard 1West 12 Tribes Chart. They are, however, included in the standard 1West Table of Nations Chart. Who, according to the 1Westers, are Indians and Pakistanis? Elamites. This means they are Gentiles according to 1West. This would be a problem for young Obama if he was an "Israelite" by the 1West definition. Since Obama's father was a Kenyan, it's not considered a problem because both Hamites and Elamites are Gentile nations.

HAMITES & CUSHITES: AFRICANS ARE NOT OUR PEOPLE

In *Barry*, young Obama has a white girlfriend, Charlotte. Charlotte is a composite character based off several of Obama's white girlfriends, such as Genevieve Cook and Alex McNear. If Obama was a "Jake", a white girlfriend would be a major problem. Since 1Westers consider Obama a "Hamite", and therefore a Gentile, it's not such a big deal. As we all know, Obama later met and married a young attorney named Michelle Robinson, who is "African-American". According to the 1West interpretation of Deuteronomy 28, Michelle Obama would probably be understood as an ethnic Israelite. Now the marriage of Barack Obama to Michelle Obama would be considered a problem since it supposedly entails people of two different nations.

To hear a 1West perspective on "interracial relationships", simply Google "IUIC" and "interracial marriage" and watch the return hits. IUIC (Israelite United in Christ) is a "Hebrew Israelite" camp descended from 1West. IUIC regularly publishes memes, lectures and videos on the topic "Interracial Marriage Is a Sin".

I have spoken with a number of people "counseled" by IUIC to dissolve their marriage after it was revealed their spouse was not an "Israelite".[13] Here is the strangest case I have heard: the woman was black and it "appeared" the man was, too, but when it was revealed that the man's mother was black but his father was white – the wife was told to divorce the man. "You are what your father is", is a "Hebrew Israelite" axiom. By this logic, the man was white, no matter what he "looked like". This axiom about the father produces strange results. For example, reggae artist Bob Marley is considered an "Edomite" because his father was not black.

IMPOSTORS, THE ASHKENAZI JEWS

Ironically, the screenwriter for *Barry* is an American Jew, Adam Mansbach. But to a "Hebrew Israelite," Adam Mansbach and those like him are the worst of the worst of the Gentiles: an imposter! An Edomite! An Amalekite! A Khazarite! One "Hebrew Israelite" author whose bio states he is "a graduate of San Francisco Theological Seminary," writes, "It is clear that most, if not all, modern-day Jews are not ancestrally or genetically linked to the house of Judah, and therefore, they have no right to be called Israelites in any sense of the word. Today's Jews are neither Judahites or Israelites. They are quite literally, masquerading imposters! Yahshuah promises to expose them and bring them down and have them acknowledge the true Hebrew-Israelites."[14] Two standard verses "Hebrew Israelites" misuse in support of this thesis are Revelation 2:9 and 3:9, where John refers to first century Jewish persecutors as the "synagogue of Satan". 1Westers claim modern day Jews (e.g., Sephardim and Ashkenazim) are not the true descendants of the ancient Hebrews. That is why so many of them look so white or European today. This passage describes this fact in the 1West opinion.[15] Those are probably the two most prominent "the modern Jews are frauds, not true Israelites" passages.

On a Google Plus post dated December 28, 2016, a user under the banner "Indigenous People of the World Unite" wrote this:

> *Barack Obama new movie on Netflix called Barry.*
> *The Hebrew Israelites are telling it like it is!*
> *Notice they didn't show the face picture of King James.*
> *Hollyweird is so full of s*** and who runs Hollyweird?*

The 1West answer to that rhetorical question is ... the Jews! Granted, it's a conspiracy trope to say Jews run Hollywood, but the "Hebrew Israelites" take it to another level: they often claim Hollywood knows the truth about the "real Jews" and is "winking" at the "Hebrew Israelites" through film.[16] Let's go back briefly to a more standard conspiracy theory, that of the Jews running the banks. "Hebrew Israelites" often reference Henry Ford to "prove" their point: "Henry Ford knew the big Ponzi scheme the elite Jewish bankers were running", writes Ronald Dalton, Jr., in *Hebrews to Negroes: Wake Up Black America*, "but the American people didn't at the time didn't see it."[17]

NO EVIDENCE? THAT'S PART OF THE COVER UP!

This is a good time to discuss conspiracy theories and the Hebrew Israelism, for they are *steeped* in them. Imagine if Alex Jones and Jerry Fletcher could be merged into one person (like the DC Comics character Firestorm) – and then when that composite conspiracy theorist emerges, add Art Bell as a third component. Now, you have the average 1Wester conspiracy theorist. A sad but humorous illustration of this occurred during a debate between James White and Elder Rawchaa. Dr. White asked for a primary source for a claim Rawchaa made. Rawchaa cited a book titled *Illuminati 2* (I never knew there was an *Illuminati 1*!). Not only is *Illuminati 2* not a primary source, it is chock full of the most wild-eyed conspiracy theories imaginable. I know: I own it and it is *bad*. The reason I cite this example is because if the undisputed leader of the second largest 1West camp cites a book like *Illuminati 2*, it's probably even worse for the average 1West member. I estimate that a significant number (a quarter?) of all 1Westers are also Flat-Earthers.

THE LANDO CALRISSIAN VERSION OF THE BIBLE[18]

Flash back to our opening springboard scene in Barry, with the 1Wester and young Obama. Let's revisit their debate. the 1Wester is insulting a drunken Caucasian woman. Young Obama is portrayed as looking on with a measure of empathy and confusion and verbally diverts the attention (and insults) away from the woman with this question and:[19]

YOUNG OBAMA: How come you're using a King James Bible?

HEBREW ISRAELITE: What?

YOUNG OBAMA: Why that edition? I thought King James was a white devil?

HEBREW ISRAELITE: Here's King James right here. Take a good look. He looks like Billy Dee Williams if you'd ask me.

YOUNG OBAMA: If you say so, brother ... *(walks away)*

HEBREW ISRAELITE: *(resumes street teaching)* Now you might ask? How did the Lost Tribes of Israel become Lost? Well, I'll tell you.

There are several notables from this slice of the script. One is the 1West notion that King James of Scotland was a "black Israelite". I can think of no better way to do this than to simply quote a "Hebrew Israelite" author on the topic:

> *I know that this image of a black King James can be a little confusing because of your Western education but this is the truth that is known by the rich and the elite of the world. That was the reason I paraded all of the English historians and professors*

> *before I got into the bowels of this book. I had to get your mind ready to receive the truth! King James came from a long line of black Scottish Stewart Kings ... the Stewarts not only ruled in Scotland they ruled France, Spain, Ireland and England/Britain/Wales. King James was able to rule all of these lands because all of these people were of Iberian (black) descent, they were the same people.*[20]

"Hebrew Israelites" often show a black and white drawing to "prove" King James was a "black Israelite". The commonly used online version is often compressed, darkened, and the dimensions have been oddly altered. An extreme close up of an unaltered, high-res version of the same drawing clearly shows King James to have fine hair and other European features. This should not be scandalous, being that he was a European king. One time a 1Wester told me that the family name (Stuart) of King James could mean "black" (I have seen no evidence of this). Ironically, the person who told me this bore the last name of WHITE (which they were not). When I pointed this out to my conversation partner, they failed to see the irony, humor, or significance of my point. It should be obvious: even if it was true that Stuart could mean "black," that does not mean he was because the person I was talking to was "black" with a last name of "white."[21] This whole claim has no historical merit. The man's lineage is widely available for all to see.

More could be said about this but instead I recommend to you the documentary film, "Black Hebrew Israelites Debunked" by Reformed Apologetic Ministries. The producer, Keith Thompson, does a fine job brining out historical facts which easily debunk the outlandish historical claims of 1Westers. (Note: my recommendation of this film does not mean I 100% co-sign every aspect of the work but I do recognize it as a helpful resource).

NOT ONLY KING JAMES BUT KING DAVID ... AND EVERYONE ELSE, TOO

"Hebrew Israelite" authors claim the ancient Hebrews were black skinned (they do not accept the designation of "dark-skinned" as accurate). For example, Rabbi Wentworth A. Matthew produced a handbook for members of his Commandment Keepers congregation in Harlem. Titled *The Anthropology of the Ethiopian Hebrew and their Relationship of the Fairer Jews*, it included the argument that Jacob and the patriarchs were black. Rebekah "brought forth twins, one red and hairy all over like a hairy garment, while the other was plain and smooth, as the black man invariably is. The first, the red and hairy one was called Esau; the plain and smooth brother was called Jacob."[22] Granted, that is a brief and somewhat undeveloped claim: Jacob was black because he was "plain and smooth". Other "Hebrew Israelite" authors make similar but more developed versions of the claim.[23]

The word translated as "red" in Genesis 25:25 (or "ruddy" in the KJV) is *admoni*. If this is an indication Esau was white (because you can see the red in white people's faces, as the argument goes), then King David was also white! 1 Samuel 17:42 uses the same word to describe David as he faced Goliath. Israelite princes are also described with this same word in Lamentations 4:7. Further, animals are described with the same word in Zechariah 1:8, Exodus 25:5 and Numbers 19:2. So are war shields in Nahum 2:3, fermented wine in Proverbs 23:31 and sin in Isaiah 1:18. The word seems to mean dark "red" or even "reddish."[24] It simply is not a word to describe so-called "white people" – it just isn't.

Although he is not an academic commentator, the historian Josephus is important in our discussion because "Hebrew Israelites" employ him regularly to "prove" their points (e.g., "Josephus said millions of Israelites fled into Africa!"). Josephus contradicts the 1West claim that Jacob was black and Esau was white:

> *"Now when the supper was got ready, he took a goat's skin, and put it about his arm, that by reason of its hairy roughness, he might by his father be believed to be Esau; for they being twins, and in all things else alike, differed only in this thing."*[25]

Josephus claims they were identical twins and the only difference between them was that Esau was hairy.

As a preliminary proof for a related argument, "Hebrew Israelite" authors explain how ancient Egyptians called their land and themselves *Khemet* (which could mean "black land" or "Land of the Black Soil").[26] From this they attempt to demonstrate that ancient Hebrews looked like Egyptians - black.[27] They may also include passages such as Psalm 78:51 and 105:23-27 which call Egypt the land or house of Ham. They claim all descendants of Ham are black-skinned. The point: the ancient Egyptians were black-skinned, and so were the ancient Israelites.[28] They buffer this with what can be classified as the "Israelite mistaken for a black Egyptian" passages.[29] For example, they claim Joseph's brothers mistook him for an Egyptian. Since the Egyptians were a black-skinned people (as the argument goes), Joseph had to be black-skinned "Since the Egyptians were Black, Joseph had to blend in with the Black-skinned Egyptians in order for his brothers not to recognize him. If Joseph were White, he would have stood out racially among the Black Egyptians."[30]

When Joseph was accused of rape in Potiphar's house, Potiphar's wife pointed out Joseph's different ethnic background: in Genesis 39:14 ("he has brought us a Hebrew to laugh at us") and again in 39:17 ("the Hebrew servant, whom you have brought among us, came in to me to laugh at me"). The Egyptians were not confused about "who was who". They knew Joseph was a Hebrew. It was enough of an issue that Potiphar's wife believed it would resonate negatively with the crowd. The chief cupbearer also referred to Joseph as a "young Hebrew" in Genesis 41:12. When Joseph's brothers came to him, they did not recognize him. He treated them as strangers and spoke to them roughly (Genesis 42:7, 30). He certainly was dressed the part of an Egyptian (Genesis 41:42) and spoke the language (Genesis 42:3).[31] Why would they expect to find the brother they sold into slavery here?

Based on Exodus 2:16-19, "Hebrew Israelites" also claim since Moses was mistaken for an Egyptian by the women he saved from raiders, Moses was black-skinned: "The young women described an 'Egyptian' as being their savior. This is because Moses was still wearing Egyptian attire, and being dressed as an Egyptian, the young women mistook him as an Egyptian. Since we know that the Egyptians were Black, we can easily assert that Moses, himself was Black. There is no way these young women would have mistaken him for an Egyptian, if he had White skin, blue eyes, and blond hair."[32] This claim is usually preceded by this slant on Exodus 2:1-10: "The fact that Moses was raised as an Egyptian already proves to us that He was black... ."[33]

A few things can be said in response to these claims about Moses being black. First, this argument depends on the mistaken assumption that ancient Egyptians were black. It is true they lived on the African continent. It is clear from all available evidence they were definitely not "white". Ancient Egyptians seem to have had a wide range of "brownish" or olive skin tones.[34]

Second, it must be remembered that when Pharaoh's daughter discovered the baby Moses, she observed: "this is one of the Hebrews' children" (Exodus 2:6-7). She seemed to know the baby was Hebrew and not Egyptian. A "Hebrew Israelite" might argue that was because the baby was circumcised. At this point, the argument is proceeding from a guess, not from evidence.[35] To solidify the point: some Egyptians practiced circumcision as well, so circumcision would not be a definitive marker.[36]

Furthermore, when Moses was 40 (Acts 7:23), the Hebrew slaves knew Moses was not an "ethnic Egyptian" (Exodus 2:14). As with Joseph, Moses most certainly was still dressed as an Egyptian. If Hebrews had a similar "color range" as the Egyptians, then the style of dress would be a clue to most people. Moses knew the Egyptian language (Acts 7:22) and may have spoken it – another clue to the women (Ex 2:17).

Another claim is that if Yahweh turned Moses' (and later his siblings) skin white as snow, then Moses must have been black. If Moses was already white-skinned, as the reasoning goes, it would not have been a miracle to turn his hand white:

> *Moses performed the second miracle in front of the Israelite elders. We are told in the Torah that there were 600,000 men amongst the Israelites. Assuming a very conservative estimate of one elder for every thousand men would give Moses an audience of at least 600 elders. The change of hand colour to white would have to be visible from a distance, given a minimum crowd of 600. A change of colour from tan to white would not be visible from the back of the crowd and would not be seen as more impressive than turning a rod into a snake. The only change of colour that could be seen by everyone in a crowd and would be more impressive than the first is a change from a black complexion to a white one.*[37]

The incident in and 4:27-31 was designed to promote belief (Exodus 4:1, 31), not to tell readers the color of Moses' skin. "Hebrew Israelite" apologists must read into the account to come up with the idea of Moses' original skin color based off the notion of what would look more spectacular to the crowd. They miss the entire flow of the passage: Aaron spoke to the people first, and then the signs were done (Exodus 4:30). Prior to this, Moses experienced it in private (4:6-7), met with his family (4:18-26), including Aaron (4:27-28), the elders of Israel (4:29), and finally, Israel proper (4:30-31). Imagine a whole swirl and building up of these displays as more and more Israelites become aware. The change from skin was not the only sign, for there were three (4:1-9). Finally, if this leprous condition turned Moses' hand stark white, this would be a phenomenon no matter what his prior skin color, for no one's skin is truly white, and this leprosy turned the skin a color resembling snow, as we see later in Numbers 12:10.[38]

To clarify: this does not mean Moses looked white or European at all. There is no way he looked like Charlton Heston, as portrayed in the *Ten Commandments* movie. Perhaps he looked more like the DreamWorks *Prince of Egypt* version of Moses? Regardless, this is not a hill to die on, but it is helpful to have some background information when talking to "Hebrew Israelites" because they are keen to bring up these questions.

"HEBREW ISRAELITE" CLAIMS REGARDING THE NEW TESTAMENT

"Hebrew Israelites" also claim Jesus Christ is described as a black man of color in several passages, such as Daniel 7:9, 10:6 and Revelation 1:13-15: "The most convincing evidence of the Messiah's color is the Biblical text. Concerning Jesus, John the Revelator writes, 'His head and his hairs were white like wool, as white a snow; and his eyes were as a flame of fire; And his feet like unto fine brass, as if they burned in a furnace; and his voice as the sound of many waters.' John describes Jesus as black with wooly hair."[39]

"Absolute Truth" is a song by St. Louis-based Christian hip hop artist Flame. In the song, Flame mentions the "Black Hebrew Israelite" interpretation of Revelation 1:14:

> *I get it – Jesus didn't have blue eyes*
> *Blonde hair, but sheep wool. Skin, bronze (Like mine)*
> *You say, "That's what the text say." I say, "Oh, we usin' the Bible?" (Oh, okay!)*

Well, let me show you what the text say / Checkmate – context is so vital
You're making reference to Revelation in Chapter 1
Verses 14 and following. The Apostle John
Gave a description of his vision of Jesus, the Son
Them characteristics represented judgment to come
And other things, But it wasn't describing his race (At all)
In that case, He literally has fire in His face
So, we cannot isolate verses and make 'em say
What we want / Warnings of that are on the last page / In that same book

To put it another way: if this a description of his ethnic features, then what race of people has swords in their mouths? If "Hebrew Israelites" want to say because his hair was white like wool that Jesus had a wooly white afro, then what do they do with the first part of the verse? "His head and his hairs were white?" His HEAD and his HAIRS were WHITE? If they want to be consistent, then Jesus must have a white head. "Hebrew Israelites" are fond of saying that Jesus had black feet and your feet must match the rest of your body. OK, then if Jesus had a head that was white, then what was the color of the rest of his body? Congratulations, "Hebrew Israelites", you just painted a picture of a white Jesus better than any Renaissance painter ever did.

The real tragedy is that the ""Hebrew Israelite" version misses the big picture: these features represent the deity of Christ. In Daniel 7:9, we read "I beheld till the thrones were cast down, and the Ancient of days did sit, whose garment was white as snow, and the hair of his head like the pure wool: his throne was like the fiery flame, and his wheels as burning fire." In Daniel, the one who is described with these features is the Ancient of Days.

1Westers turn texts about wrath into texts about race; they turn texts about deity into texts about epidermis; they turn texts about eternality into texts about ethnicity; and they turn texts about Christ into texts about color.

They also say that in Matthew 2:13, when the angel of the Lord told Joseph to hide Jesus in Egypt, they could not have blended in if they did not look like Egyptians – black-skinned. This claim is sometimes bolstered by referencing a 2001 BBC program, "The Complete Jesus". Mark Goodacre is cited as saying Jesus couldn't have hidden among Egyptians if he didn't look like them: "Now it's very unlikely that Jesus would have been able to be hidden in Egypt, if he had a very different color of skin from the people in Egypt." I have seen this quote referenced but have not been able to confirm it yet or its context. Nonetheless, notice Dr. Goodacre is not attributed as saying Jesus was black or anything like that. He just is attributed as saying Jesus would've blended in better if he looked like an Egyptian. Perhaps. All we know for sure is the child and his family were divinely protected.

The Nazis guilty of war crimes who fled to South America via "ratlines" (Nazi escape route system) did not always look like their host populations. Furthermore, Egypt was not monochromatic or ethnically homogenous. This means that even based upon this argument's internal logic (which is not 100% solid in the first place), Jesus "blending in" tells us little about what he would have looked like. Lastly, this misplaced focus misses the point: this was all done in order to fill up the full meaning of Hosea 11:1 "When Israel was a child, I loved him, and out of Egypt I called my son." In his book on themes from Matthew (God With Us), DA Carson clarifies Matthew's later use of Hosea 11:1:

> *Jesus is often presented in the New Testament as the antitype of Israel; that is, the true and perfect Israel who does not fail. ... Israel on the Old Testament is the Lord's son (Exod. 4:22, 23; Jer. 31:9); but Jesus, Himself a son of Israel, indeed a son of David, was supremely the son of God; and therefore He re-enacted or recapitulated something of the history of the "son" (the nation of Israel) whose very existence pointed forward to him.*

"Hebrew Israelites" argue from Acts 21:37-39 and 22:2-3 that the chief captain mistook Paul for an Egyptian because Paul looked like a black Egyptian: "It must be pointed out that St. Paul was black and was once mistaken for an Egyptian (Acts 21: 37-39)."[40] The mistaken assumption that Egyptians were black is still at work. Contemporaneous evidence (we can see their faces now!) suggests they were not. Funerary portraits from 1st – 3rd century Roman Egypt display a diverse array of skin shades present in Egypt. Most could be described as light brown or olive; a few could be described as black.[41] Furthermore, the chief captain's assumption about Paul had to do with potential rabble-rousing activities, not skin tone. Interestingly, once he heard Paul speak Greek, it appears he questioned his prior assumption about Paul being the Egyptian.

1WEST ESCHATOLOGY: ROLLIN' IN MY CHARIOT

1Westers believe when the United States of America falls, Christ will return and enslave all "non-Israelite" peoples. How will America fall? Nuclear winter. But how will the "Israelites" living in the US escape? Via escape ships manned by black angels. These space ships will transport 1Westers to Israel while the US is simultaneously being destroyed by nuclear missiles.[42] After these ships (from Ezekiel's vision) drop them off, they will begin their 1,000 year reign with the other nations as their slaves. At the end of the Millennium, all the "Edomites" will be annihilated. Other "non-Israelite" nations will live on via perpetual reincarnation as a permanent servant underclass for "Israel".

1Westers believe they will "roll on the nations" in UFO chariots as they kill other peoples (especially "Esau") with laser beams which emit from their eyes, and heat waves which burst forth from the chariots. They will do all this before the millennial reign. It's unclear why they will need the chariots because 1Westers believe they will fly in the Kingdom. Perhaps they will not be given their X-Men powers until after the Millennium begins? The nations (including "Esau") must survive in large part so they can go into slavery. Then, after 1,000 years of slavery, they will exterminate all white people ("Edomites"). Of course, 1Westers believe the white man is the devil and antichrist, too.

GMS doctrine that teaches rape, killing and torture will be acceptable in The Kingdom - as long as it is an "Israelite" towards a "non-Israelite". There are online videos where GMS members attempt to defend and explain the "rape doctrine". There is literally a video called "The Rape Doctrine Explained".[43] I have personally been on the receiving end of the 1West revenge fantasy. Here were some comments directed at me in the Live Video Chat of a GMS Chicago On Air Live Stream video on September 4, 2017:

"Missile food exposing themselves daily"

*"It's gone be hell for his a** in the Kingdom"*

"We gone have a party with Vocab Malone's body"

"Nah, Apostle Tahar gets Vocab Malone"

"I'll be happy to get his bones LOL"[44]

TITUS 3:9 STRIKES AGAIN

If Deuteronomy 28:68 is supposed to be a definitive proof that those who endured the Trans-Atlantic Slave Trade are descendants of Israelites, then why do some camps such as IUIC preach and teach in countries like Ghana and claim that some "Hebrew Israelites" were left behind? If this is the case, then verse 68 is not evidence of Hebrew ancestry because one can be a Hebrew without "fulfilling" it!

This sort of phenomenon relates to a dispute between the GMS Camp leadership and Zabach (a prominent veteran 1Wester). There was a video of Zabach treating a young Korean-American man as a "heathen". However, because the Korean-American carried himself in a way which imbued certain stereotypes associated with "urban swag", GMS members claimed to have "read his spirit" (through online video, no less). GMS determined that the Korean-American man was actually an "Israelite" (a "Jake"). GMS accused Zabach of being "unspiritual" and "carnal". Zabach responded by saying how the man carried himself or talked was irrelevant. Zabach offered the example of "Edomites" (white folks) who grew up around "Jakes" (black folks) and thus have that sort of "style" in how they present themselves. Zabach further noted there are "Israelites" who have "Esau's" style on them because of who they grew up around (think Carlton). This gets to the heart of the problem with the 1Wester approach:

1. *Membership in Israel is determined only by paternal lineage.*

2. *People of a single paternal lineage can instantiate a wide spectrum of morphologies.*

3. *You don't know anyone's paternal lineage for certain.*

4. *You are in no position to say who is or is not an Israelite.*

GMS's alleged ability to "read spirits" is hard to take seriously in light of how often they change decisions about a person, seemingly based on whether or not that person agrees with them. On numerous occasions, Tahar (leader of GMS) has referred to past camp members (of GMS, HODC or ICUPK) whom he now considers heathens, saying "remember so-and-so, [that Edomite, or that Hamite, or that Elamite] that used to be in the camp...?"

The psychology behind Tahar's game of ethnic musical chairs became most obvious when Tahar once addressed Nathaniel (leader of rival IUIC), saying "you better be careful, Nate, because you're starting to look like a Watusi". Per Tahar's doctrine, Nathanyel cannot do anything about his lineage. Tahar offered the warning because he meant Nathanyel better be careful about opposing him. Otherwise, Tahar might declare Nathanyel a Gentile in the recesses of his own mind, damning Nathanyel to an afterlife of eternal servitude.[44]

Vague bickering about "reading spirits" is haphazard methodology.

CHAPTER 3 ENDNOTES

1. The line about killing white babies was not a one-time slip. Captain Tazaryach has a history of hateful, murderous, and bigoted remarks. Here a few more examples: "This is why I want white people in the Kingdom. This is why I want Africans in the Kingdom. Because *I'm* not picking no grapes." – Captain Tazaryach of the ISUPK on Israelite Vibez Radio, June 30, 2016. KTL Radio: KNOW THE LEDGE RADIO w ISUPK Captain Tazaryach (#28): "I love [Khalid Muhammad] ... like I don't think there's a person that [who] hated white more people than Khalid Muhammad" – at the 1:24:13 mark. I hope that after you read the dialogue, you begin to understand the self-hatred 1Westism causes. It's the true sell-out religion. This heresy causes unbelievers (here represented by Sa Neter) to mistakenly blame God's Word on this nonsense. This is one more reason is why this doctrine is a problem.

2. They reckon this to be 1619 at Jamestown (1619-2019 or 2049).

3. This view was expressed, for example, by IUIC on an August 6, 2016 video lecture: "Why Do the Heathen Rage and the People Imagine a Vain Thing". https://youtu.be/T3sAjOqxpkg. Accessed 01/25/2017.

4. https://www.youtube.com/user/IUICintheClassRoom/videos. Accessed 9/25/17.

5. Rudolphf R. Windsor, *The Valley of the Dry Bones: The Conditions that Face Black People in America* (Atlanta, GA:Windsor's Golden Series, 1986), 96.

6. Windsor, *Dry Bones*, 98.

7. Windsor, *Dry Bones*, 101.

8. Windsor, *Dry Bones*, 101-102.

9. For a thorough commentary on this passage, see Daniel I. Block, *The Book of Ezekiel, Chapters 25-48, NICOT* (Grand Rapids, MI: Eerdmans, 1998), 367-424.

10. Iain M. Duguid, *Ezekiel: The NIV Application Commentary* (Grand Rapids, MI: Zondervan, 2009), 430.

11. Christopher J. Wright, *The Message of Ezekiel* (Downers Grove, IL: InterVarsity Press, 2001), 311.

12. Wright, *Ezekiel*, 310.

13. On IUIC's official website, there is a cautionary tale about a black woman who married a white man, "In the Storm Black Woman Gets a Reality Check" (Nov. 2012). It's a bizarre example to use against so-called "interracial marriage" because it does not appear as if the husband did anything wrong. The tragedy is how the neighbors refused to help in any way as her two young children were swept away in Superstorm Sandy. It is reported she cried in the street for twelve hours. An IUIC officer, Malachi, commented on the significance: "Apparently, a sister under the ILLUSION of marrying an Esau that she will be included". The point is that marrying a "non-Israelite" will still not "get you in good" with the other nations – especially white people. Accessed 6/9/2017.

14. John Brinson, *The Jewish Masquerade: The Relationship Between Modern Jews and Ancient Hebrew Israelites* (Denver, CO: Outskirts Press), 2010, back cover.

15. Examples of these exegetical BHI claims can be found at these websites:

http://www.stewartsynopsis.com/physical_appearance_of_ancient_i.htm

http://macquirelatory.com/Physical%20Appearence.htm

http://www.angelfire.com/il2/HebrewIsraelites3/color2.html

http://www.africason.com/2015/04/ancient-israelites-hebrews-were-black.html

16. Someone needs to write a book titled *Going to the Movies with Hebrew Israelites* and detail their theories and claims about various films.

17. Location 14606, Kindle Edition.

18. This title is a play on the "Hebrew Israelite" teacher's line that King James looked like Billy Dee Williams (who played Lando Calrissian in *The Empire Strikes Back* and *Return of the Jedi*. A different "Hebrew Israelite" believes King James looks like Mayor Dinkins. http://www.washingtoncitypaper.com/news/article/13035102/the-real-jews. Accessed 6/11/17.

19. The Coli is a well-known message board specializing in sports and hip hop. A post dated December 21, 2016 reads: "Barack Outchea Trying to Cape for a White Woman; Gets Shut Down By Black Israelites". *Cape* is slang for playing the role of hero or defender for another person. One poster approvingly quotes the "SHUT Yo MOUTH, CAVE b****" line, followed by three Michael Jordan laughing faces. Another says, "I gotta use that one".

20. Lee Cummings, *The Negro Question Part 4: The Missing Link* (CreateSpace, 2015), 8.

21. Many 1Westers black wash many historical figures, not just King James or biblical characters. For example, many claim that Abraham Lincoln was also a black Israelite.

22. Howard M. Brotz, *The Black Jews of Harlem: Negro Nationalism and the Dilemmas of Negro Leadership* (New York, NY: Schocken Books, 1964), 20.

23. Ella J. Hughley, *The Truth About Black Biblical Hebrew-Israelites* (Springfield Gardens, NY: Hughley Productions, 1982), 39-42.

24. Leonard J. Coppes, *Theological Wordbook of the Old Testament*, ed. R. Laird Harris, Gleason L. Archer, Jr. and Bruce K. Waltke, electronic ed. (Chicago: Moody Press, 1999), 11.

25. Josephus, *The Complete Works*, 18.6.

26. One "Hebrew Israelite" author does so partially on the basis of the name of ancient Egypt itself: "The ancient term for Egypt was KMT pronounced Kemet, which simply means 'THE LAND OF THE BLACKS', pointing to the rich soil of the Nile valley. What about the Bible term for the son of Noah called Ham, in Hebrew it is Kham, which has the modern Hebrew letters of חם which means Hot. Not the wording of Kmt and Khm in Hebrew they are identical words that represented the coloring of the nation of Egyptians. Now anything that remains hot for a significant period of time does not remain white in color but will eventually turn black so the meaning is implied within the letters Kmt". Rabbi Simon Altaf, *Yahushua the Black Messiah*, (n.p., Abrahamic-Faith Publishers), Kindle Location 17.

27. Sometimes they follow this up with the claim that the Bible "classifies" Ethiopians and Hebrews together, citing Amos 9:7: "Are ye not as children of the Ethiopians unto me, O children of Israel? saith the Lord".

28. As a corollary to this doctrine, "Hebrew Israelites" claim Revelation 2:9 and 3:9 prove modern day Jews are not true descendants of the ancient Hebrews. They explain that this is why so many of them look so white or European today.

29. I list a few in the main text but that list is by no means an exhaustive list of their proof texts. For example, they claim in Genesis 50:7-11, where the Canaanites who saw Jacob's funeral procession (which was a mixed company of Egyptians and Israelites) said, "this is a grievous mourning to the Egyptians." They teach this describes the Hebrews as looking like the ancient Egyptians and this means they were both black-skinned.

30. Calvin Evans, *Black Bloodlines* (n.p., Sag-gig-ga Publishing), Kindle Locations 351-353.

31. We also know Joseph spoke their language from Genesis 45:1: "Then Joseph could not control himself before all those who stood by him. He cried, 'Make everyone go out from me.' So no one stayed with him when Joseph made himself known to his brothers."

32. F. Johnson, *Truth Of Our Fathers: The Awakening Of The Hebrew Israelites* (p. 77). createspace.com. Kindle Edition.

33. Maurice Lindsay, *Wake Up To Your True Identity: Revealing The Biblical Nationality Of The So-Called African Americans* (n.p., Blessed Press), Kindle Location 14.

34. Edwin M. Yamauchi, *Africa and the Bible.* (Grand Rapids, MI: Baker Academic, 2004).

35. Furthermore, we do not know Moses was circumcised. In fact, some rabbis even argued Moses was not circumcised and therefore would not be admitted into Paradise. Then again, other rabbis argued that Moses was actually born circumcised (see these four examples: *Midrash Tanchuma, Noach, 5*;. *Avot D'Rabbi Natan 2:5*; *Talmud Sotah 12a*; *Shemot Rabbah 1:24*).

36. Gerald A. Larue, "Religious Traditions and Circumcision", paper presented at The Second International Symposium on Circumcision, San Francisco, California, April 30-May 3, 1991. http://www.nocirc.org/symposia/second/larue.html. Accessed 01/18/2017.

37. Gert Muller, *The Ancient Black Hebrews* (n.p., Pomegranate Publishing), Kindle Locations 236-240.

38. There are other, more minor, passages the "Hebrew Israelites" (and sometimes Afrocentric Bible interpreters) use to show the Ancient Israelites were black: Jeremiah 14:2, Song of Solomon 1:5, Isaiah 29:22, Lamentations 5:10, Numbers 6:5 and Judges 16:13. I do not want to cover all these in this work, because there are other, more foundational claims to discuss.

39. Elisha Israel, *Hair Like Wool, Feet Like Burned Brass: The Color of Jesus and Burning Truths Concerning the Messiah* (Kindle Locations 253-256). Elisha J. Israel Publishing L.L.C.. Kindle Edition.

40. Aylmer Von Fleischer, *The Black Role in the Bible* (n.p., n.p.), Kindle Locations 76-77.

41. "The Study and Conservation of Four Ancient Egyptian Funerary Portraits: Provenance, Conservation History and Structural Treatment". Nicola Newman, Lynne Harrison, David Thomas, Joanne Dyer and John Taylor. The British Museum Technical Research Bulletin. Volume 7, 2013. Sometimes "Hebrew Israelites" argue back and say these portraits only represent the Greek and Roman upper class or that they are all images of mixed (and therefore lighter) Egyptians. This come back cannot be proved definitively and does not have a scholarly consensus. Even if that was the case, the Chief Captain thinking Paul was an Egyptian does not mean Paul had to be black, because according to the Hebrew Israelite's own logic, many Egyptians were mixed and lighter at this time.

42. My friend Abu reminded me that once *Independence Day* came out, GMS and others started insisting that the chariots would quite suddenly upend world civilizations. This is why GMS members often hold poster boards with images from the *Independence Day* movie. In a video titled "The Most Hateful Group in America", Bay Area GMS members use a video stills from the film to encourage young pedestrians whom they view as potential converts: "Do you believe in UFO's? Do you know what they are? They're the chariots of the Heavenly Father and big black men are in there – angels. Angels are black, it's in the Bible. ... If you ever see UFO's, just know they're here for us. ... Read Ezekiel the first chapter" https://www.youtube.com/watch?v=BLb3o65q0vk. Accessed 9/6/17. Some camps also use an image from *Terminator 2: Judgment Day* where nuclear fire is melting away Sarah Connor as she holds onto a fence. Sometimes a caption with the image will read, "White folks, this is your future".

43. https://www.youtube.com/watch?v=jdlnu4clvPI. Accessed 8/28/17.

44. A GMS member even took screenshots of the comments in order to share with others:

https://docs.google.com/document/d/1sK96knCASb5yb0X1YtTLS5Npyt_ikQ0PHcpT7gi-xcw/edit?usp=sharing

45. This account of GMS, Zabach, Tahar, Nathanyel and reading spirits is courtesy of Abu Khamr.

ROLLING STONE: *Your cousin Carl is a member of the Hebrew Israelites ... how much of his theology have you embraced?*

KENDRICK LAMAR: *Everything that I say on that record is from his perspective. ... It was taking his perspective on the world and life as a people and putting it to where people can listen to it, whether you agree or you don't agree. ...*

ROLLING STONE: *So what's your idea about the idea ... that black people sre cursed by God as per Deuteronomy?*

KENDRICK LAMAR: *That s***'s truth. There's so many different ways to interpret it, but it's definitely truth when you're talking about unity in our community and some of the things we have no control over. ...*

--Rolling Stone interview with Kendrick Lamar, 8/24/17 (print edition).

DEUTERONOMY 28 & KENDRICK LAMAR

A number of celebrities have been associated with various sects of Hebrew Israelism. Some of the more well-known celebrities are Brandon T. Jackson, Chingy, Amare Stoudemarie, Shawn Stockman (Boyz II Men), Wanya Morris (Boyz II Men), Zab Judah (boxer), Lamon Brewster, Meldrick Taylor, Whitney Houston, Kodak Black, Waka Flocka, Killah Priest, Sunz of Man, Kendrick Farris, Doug E. Fresh and Antoine Dodson. One of the more recent and certainly most explicit is award-winning rap lyricist, Kendrick Lamar.

THE CURIOUS CASE OF KENDRICK LAMAR

Kendrick Lamar's Damn sold 603,000 copies its first week – his third Billboard #1 release. Kendrick is an incredible lyricist who rose to the top via creativity, talent and raw authenticity. He is the thinking Millennial's rapper. His work lends itself to theological analysis.[1] The Atlantic states his new album's "larger target" is "inescapable human sin".[2] By one count, Kendrick references Christianity an average of 74 times per full length album.[3] His certified platinum major label debut, *good kid, m.A.A.d city*, begins with a prayer:

> *Lord God / I come to you a sinner / And I humbly repent for my sins / I believe that Jesus is Lord / I believe that you raised him from the dead / I will ask that Jesus will come to my life / And be my Lord and Savior / I receive Jesus to take control of my life / And that I may live for him from this day forth / Thank you Lord Jesus for saving me with your precious blood / In Jesus' name, Amen*

The track immediately after Kendrick's "Sinner's Prayer" intro details a lust-filled relationship with "Sherane." Moral vacillation is characteristic of Kendrick's work. Kendrick calls out his own double mindedness on "For Sale?":

"I loosely heard prayers on your first album truly / Lucy don't mind, cause at the end of the day you'll pursue me".

Lucy, short for Lucifer, is a stand-in for Satan. The implication: the Devil doesn't mind if Kendrick Lamar gives a shout out to God, because Kendrick will ultimately follow a path of temptation and sin. The song ends with Kendrick musing, "the evils of Lucy was all around me, so I went running for answers." Kendrick asks these questions of "Fear":

> *Why God, why God, do I gotta suffer? / Pain in my heart, carry burdens full of struggle / why God, why God, do I gotta bleed? / every stone thrown at you, resting at my feet / why God, why God, do I gotta suffer? / earth is no more, once you burn this mother [expletive].*

Damn indicates where Kendrick believes the answers lie: Hebrew Israelism. Kendrick's new project moves from a mild form of Christian-themed spirituality to a mild form of "Hebrew Israelite"-themed spirituality: "I'm not about a religion / I'm an Israelite, don't call me black no mo", raps Kendrick on "YAH".[4] The "Hebrew Israelite" thesis is that descendants of slaves now living in the Western Hemisphere are the true biblical Israelites.[5] The movement is a theodicy (an explanation for the reality of evil in light of a good God) at its core, teaching that the low condition of African-Americans is a direct result of failing to keep Old Testament laws. Kendrick's album title is based on a "Hebrew Israelite" distinctive: black and brown people in the US are currently cursed or *damned by God*.[6] Kendrick echoes this: "Deuteronomy say that we'd all be cursed" – as does his cousin Carl Duckworth, who makes several teaching cameos.[7] Drawing from Amos, Carl says:

> *Verse two says 'you only have I known of all the families of the earth, therefore I will punish you for all your iniquities.' So until we come back to these commandments, until you come back to these commandments, we gonna feel this way, we're gonna be under this curse. Because he said he's gonna punish us. The so-called Blacks, Hispanics, and Native American Indians are the true children of Israel.*

Some media outlets noticed Kendrick's shift into Hebrew Israelism.[8] This shift from Christianity-lite to Hebrew Israelism-lite should have a chastening effect on Christians who loudly cheered for Kendrick's past work. It is refreshing to see an artist grapple with the big issues. Yet, in light of Ephesians 5:11-12, we are to "take no part in the unfruitful works of darkness, but instead expose them. For it is shameful even to speak of the things that they do in secret" – we can't forget Kendrick's music is filled with violence, illicit sex, misogyny, substance abuse, foul language, explicit imagery, braggadocio, sacrilege, and a celebration of shameful things. Sadly, the Christian observer is left with the harrowing feeling that Kendrick's journey was headed somewhere hopeful, but took an extreme wrong turn. *Damn* carries a sense of lost possibilities.

A BRIEF RABBIT TRAIL COMMENTARY ON KENDRICK LAMAR

The popularity of secular (but religiously inclined) rappers like Kendrick Lamar has brought new attention to theological concepts in hip hop. It is intriguing to see the rise of Kendrick Lamar; an artist who confusingly combines the profane and the spiritual. While it can be enlightening to hear what Kendrick says on social and spiritual issues, the open embrace of hypocrisy is not something Christians should applaud or excuse. We can use *some* aspects of his work as touch points for evangelism, all the while critiquing the hypocritical, anemic, and ungodly components to his art. Ultimately, the hypocritical and sin-glorifying aspect of this music leave the listener unfulfilled. Hip hop fans truly seeking deeper spiritual content, should check out Gospel-centered hip hop instead.

Although we must encourage Christian listeners to be cautious and discerning listeners, we also must encourage Christian listeners to be empathetic listeners.[9] For example, Kendrick mulls over his struggle with temptation and sin. His authentic admission of failure in his lyrics is laudable (Psalm 34 and 51 are the righteous models of confession). Kendrick especially proclaims a desire for justice to prevail as he witnesses injustice after injustice all around him and throughout the centuries ... yet this desire is left unfulfilled. Both themes – confession of personal sin and a desire for justice to prevail – are gospel issues. Jesus is the Savior who wipes away the guilt of sin and gives power to overcome temptation (Romans 5-6). His eternal Kingdom is a Kingdom where permanent shalom and true justice will reign (Luke 4:16-20; Revelation 21:4).[10]

Kendrick Lamar's journey into Hebrew Israelism is prototypical of its appeal for millenials. The group targets disenfranchised minorities. Many people join because they are disillusioned with their church experience.[11] Almost all I have met have been "poorly churched". Some of these churches were entertainment-driven, money-driven, or celebrity-driven.[12] Some who embrace Hebrew Israelism place a high value on Scripture and crave deeper teaching. They charge that the churches they left did not provide serious exposition, leaving them wanting.[13] "Hebrew Israelites" often say they went to churches where holiness was not valued, church discipline was non-existent and moral standards were not enforced in any meaningful way. Another problem has been the mainstream evangelical church: they have often ignored or minimized the concerns of the minorities in large American cities.[14] This applies to both historical and current realities.[15] There are some things "Hebrew Israelites" say which really are neglected truths. Here are ten:

TEN THINGS "HEBREW ISRAELITES" GET RIGHT[16]
"Black history" matters
God chose Israel
Bigotry and prejudice exist in the church
The US deserves judgment
Injustice and oppression are addressed in Scripture (and should also be addressed by the church)
False and weak teaching – like the Prosperity Gospel - is in too many pulpits
Not enough Christians know the Scripture, especially the Old Testament
Too many Christians flee from the doctrine of God as Judge
Jesus Christ was not a white man
The government is not the answer and is often the adversary

Kendrick's older cousin, who goes by Karni Ben Israel, is (was?) a member of IUIC Jacksonville (there is a strong indication Karni has have left IUIC). In a Periscope broadcast, he said this about his younger cousin: "The guy is really looking and searching for this truth. We decided to do a song ... we talked about it while back." Carl said he and Kendrick would regularly have Bible study together and that "When Deuteronomy 28 came out, it was like he was blown away, it was like — wow".[17]

THE BIG TEXT

The central thesis for Hebrew Israelite thought is that descendants of slaves in the Western Hemisphere are the true, ethnic Israelites. Deuteronomy 28 is the *locus classicus* of the "Hebrew Israelite" thesis.[18] Hebrew Israelite proponents teach that this chapter demonstrates only people identified on their "Twelve Tribes Chart" fulfill the curses of Deuteronomy 28. Hebrew Israelite author Avdiel Ben Levi writes: "The Torah is the ONLY literary work, which answers the questions of why slavery occurred, why G-d allowed it and who or what is the True National identity of the Slaves of the Trans-Atlantic Slave Trade."[19] The claim is that since his people, whom he views as the true and dark-skinned Israelites, were disobedient. Therefore they have been subjected to the curses of Deuteronomy 28.

Another author states: "Basically these curses will be upon the Children of Israel and its seed forever until the time when the Son of Man returns, Esau's seed Edom is destroyed, and the times of the Gentiles are fulfilled. The Book of Deuteronomy, Isaiah, and Ezekiel are known to be books of prophecy, meaning that these events are to happen in the future."[20] It is important to understand they believe that white people are from Esau and can be properly classified as Edomites. Furthermore, they believe no other group on earth (this includes modern Jews, whom they see as ethnically subversive frauds) fulfills the curses: "The curses in Deuteronomy 28 describe no other race of people than blacks and this can be clearly seen without a shadow of a doubt. There is no other race of people that have been the victims of all the curses."[21] They believe that only what happened to the so-called blacks of the Americas fulfills this.[22] They are essentially claiming the Bible prophesies the Trans-Atlantic Slave Trade for "Israel" in Deuteronomy 28.

Putting Deuteronomy 28 in its proper cultural context will help us interpret it better. Parallels in Ancient Near Eastern literature are noteworthy: the Hittite treaties of the second millennium BC, the

Assyrian Esarhaddon vassal treaty (672 BC) and maybe even a few places in the Law Code of Hammurabi.[23] "The vassal treaty was employed within the Near East when a great power (the suzerain king) imposed certain conditions of vassaldom on a smaller state (the vassal)," one commentator writes, and the "Hebrews adapted the treaty form for their own use in order to express the nature of their relationship to God ... while other small states might serve Egypt or the Hittite Empire as vassals, the Israelites owed their allegiance only to their suzerain God."[24]

As alluded to earlier in this chapter, Deuteronomy 28 is the Blessing and Curse section, and verses 15-68 are called "The Warning" (*Tachacha* in Hebrew) by Jews.[25] "Hebrew Israelites" are mistaken to label this chapter "prophecy" or a textual key for determining who the true nation of Israel is, should they somehow forget their identity. "Hebrew Israelites" need to see chapter 28 for what it is, not employ it in a manner never intended. Nonetheless, some of the curses have come to pass in Hebrew history. We need not jump to the Trans-Atlantic Slave Trade to find "fulfillment" of the curses.

For example, one could say the curse of Deuteronomy 28:49, which is, "The LORD will bring a nation against you from afar, from the end of the earth, as the eagle swoops down, a nation whose language you shall not understand" was fulfilled in Hosea 8:1: "Put the trumpet to your lips! Like an eagle26 the enemy comes against the house of the LORD, because they have transgressed My covenant And rebelled against My law." The enemy is described as distant and striking swiftly as a bird of prey. This is exactly what Assyria did to Israel in 722 BC. Additionally, Isaiah 28:11 and 33:19 reference Deuteronomy 28:49 being fulfilled by the Babylonians in 605 BC, when they deported Judah: "The foreign nation would have a language not understandable to the Israelite population. Though the languages of Assyria and Babylon were cognate Semitic languages, they differed from Hebrew sufficiently so as to not be understood by the populace in Israel."[27]

Another example is the curse found in Deuteronomy 28:53: "Then you shall eat the offspring of your own body, the flesh of your sons and of your daughters whom the LORD your God has given you, during the siege and the distress by which your enemy will oppress you." It seems it was fulfilled in 2 Kings 6:24-31, which details cannibalism during the Siege of Samaria. Lamentations 2:20 and 4:10 contain a lament for the cannibalism that occurred during the Fall of Jerusalem in 586 BC. There are more intra-biblical demonstrations of the curses coming to pass in Israelite history.[28] The case can be strengthened by going to extra-biblical sources containing Jewish history.[29]

13 QUESTIONS FOR INTERPRETERS WHO ADOPT THE TRANSATLANTIC SLAVE TRADE ISRAELITE EQUIVALENCY THESIS

1. Who was the king the Israelites on the West Coast of Africa set over them who went with them through the Middle Passage?
2. Did slave traders besiege walled cities or fortified walls?
3. The first two references to Egypt in Deut. 28 are clearly literal, referring to the actual place. Why would the meaning of Egypt switch to mean "America" the third time the word appears in the same passage?
4. Why couldn't a Kenyan - who lived under British Imperialist Colonialism - also claim this passage applies to his historical lot, and that he is therefore cursed because he is an Israelite?
5. Why does verse 68 switch from literal ships to metaphorical Egypt back to literal slavery and then going back to metaphorical buying (as in "no one will redeem you")?
6. What is the objective justification for using Deuteronomy 28 as a Scriptural DNA test? Meaning, the passage is a list of punishments which will befall Israel if they violate the terms of the covenant. There is no indication it was intended to act as a way for Israel to rediscover its heritage should they forget who they were. What precept is there to show your use is in accordance with its original design?

7. How is it possible to be cursed under the law when Galatians 3 says all those who are in Christ have been freed from the curse of the law?
8. 28:46 says "these will be a sign and a wonder against you and your offspring forever". If it's a sign to Israel forever, how could they not recognize it and not know they are Israel?
9. Why doesn't this passage mention the ultimate curse: Israel will forget her identity?
10. Why does the chart switch back and forth from ethnic groups to geographical locations?
11. How are all Native Americans from Gad except Seminoles who are said to be of Ruben?
12. Many modern Mexicans are *mestizos*, which means a mix between Spaniards (Europeans) and natives! Since chart adherents believe the "Israelite" lineage must be on the father's side, how can a chart adherent differentiate between Mexicans who had Spanish *conquistador* fathers and which Mexicans had native fathers?[30]
13. If Israel is supposed to be scattered all over the world, then why does the 12 Tribes Chart only contain locations and peoples on the Western Hemisphere of the globe?

CHAPTER 4 ENDNOTES

1. Ralph Bristout, "The Book of K. Dot: Exploring the Religious Themes Tucked in Kendrick Lamar's Catalog," *Revolt*, https://revolt.tv/stories/2017/04/13/book-dot-exploring-religious-themes-tucked-kendrick-lamars-catalog-07008acdf9, accessed 4/20/2017.

2. Spencer Kornhavber, "Kendrick Lamar's Complicated Score Settling," *The Atlantic*, https://www.theatlantic.com/entertainment/archive/2017/04/kendrick-lamar-damn-politics-fox-trump/523059, accessed 4/20/2017.

3. "Kendrick Lamar, By the Numbers," *Complex Music*, April 7, 2017, http://www.complex.com/music/2017/04/kendrick-lamar-by-the-numbers, accessed 4/20/2017.

4. Kendrick now uses "Yah" for God and "Yeshua" for Jesus. Previously, Kendrick was fine with "God" and "Jesus". As he moves from being influenced by Christian concepts to Black Hebrew Israelite concepts, it follows he would share their tendency to use Hebrew.

5. The *Christian Research Journal* covered this phenomenon in an excellent article by Jimmy Butts: "The Origin and Insufficiency of the Black Hebrew Israelite Movement", Volume 39, Number 4, 2016.

6. For a standard "Hebrew Israelite" presentation, see Rudolph R. Windsor, *The Valley of the Dry Bones* (Atlanta, GA: Windsor's Golden Series), 1986.

7. Kendrick's cousin, Carl Duckworth, is a member of a Black Hebrew Israelite group known as Israel United in Christ (IUIC). Sam Kestenbaum, "EXPLAINED: Kendrick Lamar's Hebrew Israelite

Connection," *The Forward*, http://forward.com/news/369749/explained-rapper-kendrick-lamars-hebrew-israelite-connection, accessed 5/14/2017.

8. Sam Kestenbaum, "Kendrick Lamar Goes Hebrew Israelite on 'Damn'," *The Forward*, April 14, 2017, http://forward.com/fast-forward/369068/is-rapper-kendrick-lamar-a-hebrew-israelite-like-amare-stoudemire, accessed 4/20/17.

9. An excellent example is Shai Linne's, "Are Chance the Rapper and Color Book Christian Rap," Shai Linne, http://rapzilla.com/rz/features/15128-shai-linne-are-chance-the-rapper-coloring-book-christian-hip-hop?showall=1&limitstart= , accessed 5/29/17.

10. Thank you to Pastor Eric Mason, Shai Linne, and R.A. Sheats for the valuable input on the section about Kendrick Lamar.

11. A typical example is Chapter 18 of *The Hebrew Israelite Manifesto*, titled: "Doom to You Shepherds of Israel". Two excerpts should suffice. The author, speaking of the modern church and its pastors, says: "I have never witnessed so many dumb sheep that do not know the Word of God". Later, after calling Christian pastors "dumb" and "foolish", he says: "So much is at stake in this hour that if the shepherds of Israel do not get on board with the plan of God, we are about to see some heads roll". Prophet Travis Refuge, *The Hebrew Israelite Manifesto: Operation, Let My People Go!* (n.p., n.p., 2015), 234-243.

12. A common type of social media post from those who identify as "Hebrew Israelites" consists of a picture or video featuring a prosperity gospel teacher engaged in antics. The image is then followed by a variation of this statement: "why I don't go to church anymore" or "this is why I left your church".

13. Some of these considerations are discussed in Eric C. Redmond's *Where Are all the Brothers?* (Wheaton, IL: Crossway, 2008).

14. Harlem gang member turned Christian evangelist Tom Skinner pointed this out to evangelicals back in the 60s and 70s. For example, see his book *How Black is the Gospel?* (New York: JB Lippincott, 1970).

15. Black Empowerment Radio discussed these issues in-depth on their October 19, 2016 broadcast: https://youtu.be/ZDNQ_CMNgV8. Accessed 1/25/2017.

16. BEC Member Alfredo Valentin and I discussed these tent things in-depth in this video: https://www.youtube.com/watch?v=2WA4J66AwKc. Accessed 9/6/17.

17. Read more at http://forward.com/news/371315/how-kendrick-lamar-was-blown-away-by-hebrew-israelite-beliefs/

18. A case study is Nathanyel's (Israel United in Christ) opening statement in a debate with a few pastors and a college president. Nathanyel spent the bulk of his time comparing Deuteronomy 28 with the plight of black people over the past 400 years: https://www.youtube.com/watch?v=z4D26ukAN-g. Accessed August 22, 2016.

19. Adviel Ben Levi, *It Was Written and Engraved: A Series of Essays on Torah: From the Blueprint of Creation to the Trans Atlantic Slave Trade* (San Bernadino, CA: n.p.. 2016), 91.

20. Dalton Jr., Ronald, *HEBREWS TO NEGROES: Wake Up Black America* (Kindle Locations 4010-4012). G Publishing LLC. Kindle Edition.

21. Ronald Dalton, Jr. HEBREWS TO NEGROES: Wake Up Black America (G Publishing LLC., Kindle Edition), Locations 4112-4113. The same author continues with a list drawn from the passage, saying, "Here are key points and examples that you can clearly see:"

22. The importance of Deuteronomy 28 in Hebrew Israelism can be seen in the 257-page book written by Yeshiah Yisrael titled *Deuteronomy 28:15-68: The Condition of the Blacks: History Untold to the Masses* (n.p., Danite Publications), 2016.

23. Peter C. Craige, *The Book of Deuteronomy*, (Grand Rapids, MI: Eerdmans, 1976), 339-340. The point is not which came first, per se, but that understanding similar documents from the ANE helps illumine the book, especially chapter 28. Scholars such as Thompson, Mendenhall, Kitchen, and Kline all have done good work detailing the similarities.

24. Ibid., 23.

25. L. Thomas Holdcroft, *The Pentateuch*, (Abbotsford, BC: CeeTeC Publishing), 273.

26. For the first two Scriptures, I used the NASB95 because the ESV translates Hosea 8:1 as "vulture" instead of "eagle", even though the Hebrew word – *naser* - is the same in both places.

27. Earl S. Kalland, *The Expositor's Bible Commentary, Volume 3*, (Grand Rapids, MI: Zondervan, 1992), 174. Paul also quotes Isaiah 28:11-12 in 1 Corinthians 14:21.

28. For example, one can possibly cross-reference the "fierce looking nation" of 28:50 with the "stern-faced king" of Daniel 8:23. It is possible to do the same thing with the locusts of 28:38 with how the Midianites and Amalekites are described as swarms of '*arbeh*' (locusts) in Judges 6:5 and 7:12.

29. For a detailed exegesis on verse 68, see Rabbi Asher Meza's two videos "The Original Jews Were Not White" https://www.youtube.com/watch?v=LaWimz6Qano and "Deut. 28:68 Disproving the Black Hebrew Israelites" https://www.youtube.com/watch?v=HmgfajXyC6Y. Accessed 09/04/2016.

30. As a related question: how would the original Aztecs (ancestors to SOME modern Mexicans) fulfill the Deuteronomy 28 curses when they had a massive successful empire?

ELDER RAWCHAA: *Well, you know what would help? It would help if you would yield and actually give the floor back and give our Scriptures back.*

JAMES WHITE: *I'm sorry, they're not your Scriptures, sir. They were given to the Christian church as a whole.*

ELDER RAWCHAA: *James, listen: these Scriptures were given through inspiration of our prophets. These are our forefathers – my forefathers.*

JAMES WHITE: *That's your assertion.*

ELDER RAWCHAA: *That's my assertion. And guess what? You have no authority to tell me what's in this Book.*

--Debate between Elder Rawchaa of GOCC and Dr. James White, 6/29/16

RELEVANT BIBLICAL PASSAGES

In Alan Gomes' book, *Unmasking the Cults*, he lists nineteen theological characteristics of cults. About fifteen of these are true of 1West Hebrew Israelism. Three of these directly relate to how 1Westers mishandle the Word of God:

1. *Redefinition of biblical terminology*

2. *Disregard for sound hermeneutical principles*

3. *Tendency to see Scripture as alluding to their cultic movement*

In his classic book, *Kingdom of the Cults*, Walter Martin wrote, "Let it never be forgotten that cultists are experts at lifting texts out of their respective contexts, without proper concern for the laws of language or the established principles of 'Biblical interpretation". 1Westers certainly are guilty of this charge. 1Westers are certainly repeat offenders of the three crimes listed above as they read and misinterpret the Word of God. In the future and final edition of this work (this version is a limited run, abridged, pre-release test run), this chapter of the book will be longer and more detailed. Right now, it only deals with a few passages, and in a relatively limited way. Please understand this is the least developed section but that will change in the future.

Many of the 1West Bible distortions have been refuted online. Specifically, the Google Hangouts organized by members of the Shield Squad and Soldiers of God crews and in debates between "Hebrew Israelites" and Christians on Debate Talk 4U hosted by Sal Showtime. Below are the top twenty debates (in no particular order) on Scriptural topics you should hear to hear proper refutation of Hebrew Israelism styled eisegesis. Let me add a caveat: the list below does not mean I agree with every point made by the Christian debater. It simply means it is good for you to hear to become equipped with some proper arguments and counterarguments in relationship. These debates can all be found at blogtalkradio.com/debatetalk4u as well as on the show's YouTube page. Each entry lists the Christian debater's name first, the "Hebrew Israelite" debater second.

TOP 20 DEBATES ON DEBATE TALK 4U REFUTING HEBREW ISRAELISM

1. *Is Circumcision of the Flesh Needed for Salvation?*(Brother J v Israel Doctrine)
2. *Physical Resurrection: Fact or Fiction?* (G. Kon v Yahshuwah Yisrael)
3. *Do We Have to Keep Sabbath and Dietary Law?* (Bro Marcus v Robert Reed)
4. *Is the Messiah God?* (G Man v Yahshuwah Ben Yahudah)
5. *Is the White Man the Devil?* (G Man v The Shut Em Down Crew)
6. *How Do We Keep the New Covenant?* (Brother Marcus v MaQaWar Horn)

7. *The Virgin Conception: Is It Biblical?* (Vekyl v Yahshuwah Ben Israel)
8. *Who is the Kingdom of Heaven For?* (Soldiers of God v Shut Em Down Crew)
9. *Should Believers be Torah Observant?* (Ssoreal v Brother Jason)
10. *Who is Salvation For?* (Faithful to God v Ahmayan)
11. *Deuteronomy 28 Debate* (G. Kon v Moreh Yisrael)
12. *Isaiah 53 Dialogue* (G. Kon v Chris Harris)
13. *Did Paul Teach Against the Law of Moses?* (Ssoreal v Yahuchanan)
14. *Similarities and Differences Dialogue* (Vocab Malone v Zaydok Ben Israel)
15. *Similarities and Differences Dialogue* (Vocab Malone v Neo Ahdiala)
16. *Similarities and Differences Dialogue* (Vocab Malone v Brother Alvin)
17. *Breaking Down Deuteronomy 28* (with Brother Faithful to God and G. Kon)
18. *Do We Have to Keep the Law of Moses to be Saved?* (Bro J v Ahmayan)
19. *Is There a Trinity According to Scripture?* (Cleveland Jones v Ahmayan)
20. *Does Jesus Fit the Prophecies?* (Soldiers of God v Torah Knights Crew)

OBADIAH 1:15-18

Later on in the chapter, I will provide more links to online resources refuting Hebrew Israelism eisegesis. For now, let me give one example of a 1Wester who asked me to interpret a passage. Here is what he asked me (I edited grammatical for ease of reading):

> *Vocab Malone, break down Malachi 1:1-5, Obadiah 1:9-10, and ESPECIALLY Obadiah 1:15-18? If God said he hates Esau and he would be angry with them FOREVER, and there would be not one remaining of them ... how can they be included in salvation? When the Bible says WHOSOEVER calleth on the name of the Lord shall be saved, clearly, an Edomite is not included in the WHOSOEVER. Right???*

I responded like this:

> *I'm not going do this all day, where you guys, while offering NO INTERPRETATION of your own, say, INTERPRET THESE VERSES! And of course, since you have your own theological agenda, will never accept true exegesis unless the Lord opens your eyes. But here is a sample of how to approach these passages.*

Here is the text of Obadiah 1:15-18 from the English Standard Version:

> **15** *For the day of the LORD is near upon all the nations. As you have done, it shall be done to you; your deeds shall return on your own head.*
>
> **16** *For as you have drunk on my holy mountain, so all the nations shall drink continually; they shall drink and swallow, and shall be as though they had never been.*
>
> **17** *But in Mount Zion there shall be those who escape, and it shall be holy, and the house of Jacob shall possess their own possessions.*
>
> **18** *The house of Jacob shall be a fire, and the house of Joseph a flame, and the house of Esau stubble; they shall burn them and consume them, and there shall be no survivor for the house of Esau, for the LORD has spoken.*

The main point of this passage is that all nations, all people, will face God's judgment. These verses look forward to a time when Yahweh sets the world right. Man's rebellion and all oppression will be vanquished. God's people will participate in this final victory.

VERSE 15

The Day of the Lord affects all nations, of which Edom is a representative of. The representation can be seen through the linguistic connection in Hebrew: Edom and humanity are comprised of the same consonants. For example, Amos 9:12 in the LXX (Septuagint) is used by the Jerusalem Council in Acts 15:17 to make an argument for allowing Gentiles in the new church.

VERSE 16

Psalm 75:8-9, 60:3-4 and Isaiah 51:22 are good parallels to this cup of wrath imagery. This has even more import for the Christian because they see the words of Christ in Mark 14:36 and 10:38, where Christ speaks of taking the cup of wrath on himself. This means he drank the cup of God's wrath for his people; wrath was poured out on Christ instead of his elect.

VERSE 17

Obadiah's vision of a new Yahweh-led obedient community is the same theme Peter expresses in1 Peter 5:10.

VERSE 18

1:18 reflects God's final judgment of the wicked, not only Edom. This can be seen by the similar language from Exodus 15:7, against Egypt, and Isaiah 10:17 and 29:5, which are against the Assyrians. John the Baptist uses similar "fire and stubble" imagery against the Jews of his day in Matthew 3:12 and Luke 3:17.

One reason Edom received "extra" punishment was because Edom had an "extra" obligation to Judah, due to their shared ancestry. Instead,

Edom laughed at his brother Judah in 587 BC. Edom's defeat is a prelude to the overthrow of all wicked powers. Some of this prophecy was fulfilled when John Hyrcabus conquered Edom in the 2nd century BC. Judah even forced the Edomites to be circumcised and, in the words of one commentator, "deprived them of their nationhood".

OBADIAH 1:9-10

Going back earlier in the chapter, here is the ESV text of Obadiah 1:9-10 and some helpful interpretative notes.

> **9** *And your mighty men shall be dismayed, O Teman, so that every man from Mount Esau will be cut off by slaughter.*
>
> **10** *Because of the violence done to your brother Jacob, shame shall cover you, and you shall be cut off forever.*

The main point of these verses is that Edom should have had a brotherly bond to Israel but instead became an enemy and was judged.

VERSE 9

Edom's soldiers are terrified due to the catastrophe around them. Both military and civilians are killed, probably by the nations mustered against them.

VERSE 10

Edom's (represented figuratively as Esau) sins are against his brother, Jacob. Because Edom was violent, violence will come upon Edom. Edom is deprived now of both honor and pride. The destruction is total and therefore there is no hope for restoration.

MALACHI 1:1-5

The last passage the 1Wester asked me about was Malachi 1:1–5. Here is the text:

> **1** *The oracle of the word of the LORD to Israel by Malachi.*
>
> **2** *"I have loved you," says the LORD. But you say, "How have you loved us?" "Is not Esau Jacob's brother?" declares the LORD. "Yet I have loved Jacob*
>
> **3** *but Esau I have hated. I have laid waste his hill country and left his heritage to jackals of the desert."*
>
> **4** *If Edom says, "We are shattered but we will rebuild the ruins," the LORD of hosts says, "They may build, but I will tear down, and they will be called 'the wicked country,' and 'the people with whom the LORD is angry forever.'"*
>
> **5** *Your own eyes shall see this, and you shall say, "Great is the LORD beyond the border of Israel!"*

Yahweh reminds Israel of her history and their covenant together. Jacob and his line are chosen by God. Edom's place of refuge will become a wasteland instead. This is due to wickedness (3:15, 19). The hatred spoken of here denotes a lack covenant relationship. This can be seen in divorce documents (Hosea 9:15).

The same term (hate) applied to Edom here is also applied to Israel in Jeremiah 12:8 and Hosea 9:15. To reiterate, Yahweh is said to hate *Israel* in both Jeremiah 12:8 ("My heritage has become to me like a lion in the forest; she has lifted up her voice against me; therefore I hate her.") and Hosea 9:15 ("Every evil of theirs is in Gilgal; there I began to hate them. Because of the wickedness of their deeds I will drive them out of my house. I will love them no more; all their princes are rebels.").

What does this mean for Yahweh's hatred towards other nations at other points in Scripture? God's prophets often used strong language to express his hatred for sin. Sometimes these expressions are called "rhetorical Hebraisms". Yet, other passages express Yahweh's continued love for Israel (Jeremiah 12:15) as well as for other people he has created (Isaiah 56:6-8). If God can say he hates Israel in her sin in this manner, then it follows Yahweh means the same thing or at least something similar when he says he hates Edom. Additionally, Yahweh had already commanded Israel to love the Edomites in Deuteronomy 23:7: "You shall not abhor an Edomite, for he is your brother. You shall not abhor an Egyptian, because you were a sojourner in his land".

It is true that only Israel is partner in the covenant at Sinai but Esau and other nations are included in the covenant with Noah and his descendants (Genesis 9:9-10). The same thing can be seen in Genesis 36, where Esau's genealogy is included. Amos includes some Edomites in greater Israel in 9:11-12. Later, in the New Covenant, Acts 15:16-18 makes use of this fact.

An interpretation closer to the actual biblical meaning will not appear as "romantic" to the average 1Wester. Unless the Holy Spirit is drawing the 1Wester to true gospel repentance, he will usually be "disappointed" with any Christocentric understanding of the text. Usually, a more careful handling of the passage will not be attractive to a 1Wester.

GOD'S PEOPLE ARE (AND HAVE BEEN) MADE UP OF A MIXED MULTITUDE

Now is a good place in this work to establish a biblical foundation for an element of the New Covenant: the gospel is Good News to all those whom believe – the elect from every nation. To do this I am simply going to place a lot of Scripture which show the precedent from the

Hebrew Scriptures (Old Testament). Here are four truths which I would like to share with you and then I will give passages to back up each point:

1. Strangers had to keep covenant law, including circumcision, Passover

2. Israel was commanded to love the stranger

3. Non-Israelites could be part of God's people

4. There are multiple examples of non-Israelites being part of Israel

STRANGERS HAD TO KEEP THE COVENANT LAW, INCLUDING CIRCUMCISION, PASSOVER

Example 1: Exodus 20:10

> *But the seventh day* is *the sabbath of the LORD thy God:* in it *thou shalt not do any work, thou, nor thy son, nor thy daughter, thy manservant, nor thy maidservant, nor thy cattle,* ***nor thy stranger that*** **is** ***within thy gates.***

Example 2: Numbers 15:15

> **15** *One ordinance* shall be both *for you of the congregation,* ***and also for the stranger that sojourneth*** **with you***, an ordinance for ever in your generations:* ***as ye*** **are*****, so shall the stranger be before the LORD****.*
>
> **16** *One law and one manner shall be for you,* ***and for the stranger that sojourneth with you****.*

Example 3: Leviticus 24:10-23

The passage is too long to share in its entirety. It is significant because a son whose father was an Egyptian received capital punishment for blasphemy (Leviticus 24:10, 13, 16). This shows equal application of covenant stipulations to Israelites of "mixed ancestry", including one who had an Egyptian father. This is important because 1Westers say "you are what your father is". This means, for example, the actress who played Hilary Banks (Karyn Parsons) in Fresh Prince would not be considered an "Israelite" since her father was white (her mother was black). This passage also shows that non-Israelites were part of Israel, possibly an Egyptian man and definitely a part-Egyptian Israelite.

The King James Version translation is interesting because it reads "the son of an Israelitish woman". The Hebrew simply means "female Israelite" but the KJV translates it as "Israelitish". Well, many 1Westers use the argument that Jews are called Jewish because they are "Jew-ish", as in, sort of like a Jew but not really a true Jew.

To illustrate, "Hebrew Israelite" rappers Obadiah and Crunk God Euro have a song called "Jew", where they rap:

> *I feel like my whole life / my people been lied to / ay you can hate me for the truth / they hated on Christ, too / ain't nothing –ish about this Jew.*

It has been pointed out to 1Westers that British or Scottish people aren't sort of British or sort of Scottish! Still, since 1Westers are also usually KJV-Onlyists, the translation of the word "Israelitish" is a problem for their argument against Jews being real Jews because they are called Jewish, since the word "Israelitish" appears in their preferred translation.

Of course, I do not buy The 1West argument about the –ish suffix. I am using a presuppositional argument wherein I examine their worldview and then turn two conflicting premises they hold to against each other. One key verse out of the section above is Leviticus 10:22, which says, "Ye shall have one manner of law, as well for the stranger, as for one of your own country: for I am the LORD your God".

Example 4: Exodus 12:38, 47, 48, 49

> **38** *A* ***mixed multitude*** *went up also with them; and flocks, and herds, even very much cattle.*
>
> **47** *All t****he congregation of Israel*** *shall keep it.*
>
> **48** *And when a* ***stranger*** *shall sojourn with thee,* ***and will keep the passover*** *to the LORD,* ***let all his males be circumcised****, and then* ***let him come near and keep it****; and he shall be* ***as one that is born in the land****: for no uncircumcised person shall eat thereof.*
>
> **49** ***One law*** *shall be to him that is homeborn, and* ***unto the stranger that sojourneth*** *among you.*

To understand the context, it is best to read the whole chapter (at least). But the above verses are especially noteworthy. If you are a stranger who travels with Israel and are circumcised, you keep the Passover. This also shows the mixed multitude (Israelites and non-Israelites) includes previously uncircumcised males.

Example 5: Deuteronomy 31:12

> *Gather the people together, men, and women, and children,* ***and thy stranger that*** is ***within*** *thy gates, that they may* ***hear****, and that they may* ***learn****, and* ***fear the LORD your God****, and* ***observe to do all the words of this law.***

ISRAEL WAS COMMANDED TO LOVE THE STRANGER

Example 1: Leviticus 19:33

> **33** *And if a stranger sojourn with thee in your land,* ***ye shall not vex him****.*

> **34** But ***the stranger that dwelleth with you shall be unto you as one born among you, and thou shalt love him as thyself****; for ye were strangers in the land of Egypt: I* am *the LORD your God.*

Example 2: Deuteronomy 10:17-19

> **17** *For the LORD your God is God of gods, and Lord of lords, a great God, a mighty, and a terrible,* **which regardeth not persons**, *nor taketh reward:*

> **18** *He doth execute the judgment of the fatherless and widow, and* ***loveth the stranger****, in giving him food and raiment.*

> **19** ***Love ye therefore the stranger****: for ye were strangers in the land of Egypt.*

Example 3: Deuteronomy 23:7-8

> **7** *Thou shalt* ***not abhor an Edomite****; for* **he** is ***thy brother****: thou shalt* ***not abhor an Egyptian****; because thou wast a stranger in his land.*

> **8** ***The children that are begotten of them shall enter into the congregation of the LORD*** *in their third generation.*

Example 4: Jeremiah 22:3

Thus saith the LORD; Execute ye judgment and righteousness, and deliver the spoiled out of the hand of the oppressor: and ***do no wrong, do no violence to the stranger****, the fatherless, nor the widow, neither shed innocent blood in this place.*

NON-ISRAELITES COULD BE PART OF THE GOD'S PEOPLE

Example 1: Jeremiah 12:16-17

16 *And it shall come to pass,* ***if they will diligently learn the ways of my people****, to swear by my name, The LORD liveth; as they taught my people to swear by Baal;* ***then shall they be built in the midst of my people****.*

17 *But if they will not obey, I will utterly pluck up and destroy that nation, saith the LORD.*

Example 2: Isaiah 56:3, 6-7

3 *Let not* ***the foreigner who has joined himself to the LORD*** *say, "The LORD will surely separate me from his people"; and let not the eunuch say, "Behold, I am a dry tree."*

6 *"And the* ***foreigners who join themselves to the LORD****, to minister to him, to love the name of the LORD, and to be his servants, everyone who keeps the Sabbath and does not profane it, and holds fast my covenant—*

7 *these I will bring to my holy mountain, and make them joyful in my house of prayer; their burnt offerings and their sacrifices will be accepted on my altar; for* ***my house shall be called a house of prayer for all peoples****."*

Example 3: Ezekiel 47:22-23 "as a native-born"

22 *And it shall come to pass,* that *ye shall divide it by lot for an inheritance unto you,* ***and to the strangers that sojourn among you****, which shall beget children among you: and* ***they shall be unto you as born in the country among the children of Israel****; they shall have* ***inheritance*** *with you among the tribes of Israel.*

23 *And it shall come to pass,* that *in what tribe the* ***stranger sojourneth****, there shall ye* ***give*** **him** ***his inheritance****, saith the Lord GOD.*

Example 4: Acts 15:14-20

14 *Simeon hath declared* ***how God at the first did visit the Gentiles, to take out of them a people for his name****.*

15 *And to this agree the words of the prophets; as it is written,*

16 *After this I will return, and will build again the tabernacle of David, which is fallen down; and I will build again the ruins thereof, and I will set it up:*

17 *That the residue of men might seek after the Lord,* ***and all the Gentiles, upon whom my name is called****, saith the Lord, who doeth all these things.*

18 *Known unto God are all his works from the beginning of the world.*

19 *Wherefore my sentence is, that we trouble not them,* ***which from among the Gentiles are turned to God****:*

20 *But that we write unto them, that they abstain from pollutions of idols, and* from *fornication, and* from *things strangled, and* from *blood.*

Example 5: 2 Chronicles 6:32-33

32 *Moreover concerning* ***the stranger, which is not of thy people Israel, but is come from a far country for thy great name's sake****, and thy mighty hand, and thy stretched out arm;* ***if they come and pray in this house****;*

33 *Then hear thou from the heavens, even from thy dwelling place, and* ***do according to all that the stranger calleth to thee for****; that* ***all people of the earth may know thy name****, and fear thee, as doth thy people Israel, and may know that this house which I have built is called by thy name.*

THERE ARE MULTIPLE EXAMPLES OF NON-ISRAELITES BEING PART OF ISRAEL (AND WORSHIPPING THE GOD OF ISRAEL)

1. Caleb the Kennizite *(Genesis 15:19; Numbers 32:12; Joshua 14:6, 14)*

2. Uriah the Hittite *(2 Samuel 11:3–26, 12:9–10, 15)*

3. Naaman the Syrian *(2 Kings 5:1–23; Luke 4:27)*

4. Ebed-Melech the Ethiopian *(Jeremiah 38:7)*

5. Ruth the Moabitess *(Ruth 1:4, 6–18, 22–2:23, 3:9, 4:1–13; Matthew 1:5)*

6. Canaanite widow from Zarephath *(1 Kings 17:8-16; Luke 4:26)*

7. Rahab of Jerhico *(Josh 2:1–24, 6:1–27, Matt 1:5, Heb 11:31, James 2:25)*

REVELATION 13:9-1

Revelation 13:9-10 is a proof text for Hebrew Israelism eschatology. A perfect example is in the "Hebrew Israelite" book *The Prophecies: The Book of the Hebrew Israelites* by J.R. Willis. Here is his "breakdown" of Revelation 13:9-10 (I am recreating the text word for word, including the overuse of caps. Below is how it actually and precisely reads):

> *He that leadeth into captivity shall go into captivity-(THE BLOODLY BARBARIC TRANS-ATLANTICSLAVE TRADE THEY TOOK OUR PEOPLE INTO-100 + MILLION HEBREWS DIED-FACT-UPON CHRIST GREAT RETURN EDOM 90 PERCENT OF EDOM SHALL DIE 7 THE REMAINING CAUCASIAN SHALL BECOME SERVANTS TO THE CHILDREN OF ISRAEL, YES BLACK PEOPLE YOU SHALL OWN THEM & THOSE WHO SHALL FIGHT AGAINST THE LORD'S GREAT WILL SHALL PERISH): he that killeth with the sword must be killed with the sword-(EDOMS SATANIC WARS OF CONTINUOUS DEATH AGAINST OUR PEOPLE, THE ISRAELITES) . Here is the patience and the faith of the saints-(THE SAINT OUR GOD'S TRUE PEOPLE WHO ARE THE POOR BLACK AND BROWN PEOPLE SCATTERED AMONG THE FOUR CORNERS OF THE EARTH & ARSERETH WHICH IS THE AMERICAS). FOR BLOOD MUST BE PAID WITH BLOOD AND GREAT FATHER AHAYAH NEVER FORGETS, FOR JUDGEMENT COMES FOR ESAU WHO IS EDOM WHICH ARE THE CAUCASIAN NATIONS. DO NOT CALL IT HATE, CALL IT THE TRUTH AND THE WORD OF THE TRUE LIVING GOD OF THE HEBREWS, GREAT HOLY FATHER AHAYAH, AMEN NOW WHO SHALL DENY THIS REPORT? J.R.WILLIS AUTHOR: A RACE OF DEMONS REFINED 2017 AUTHOR: SPIRITUAL CRIMES 2018 AUTHOR: THE PROPHECIES PREPARE SLAUGHTER FOR HIS CHILDREN*[1]

The author is saying that because white people (Esau or the Edomites) took part in the Slave Trade, then white people will be made slaves, according to this passage in Revelation. Here is the KJV text of Revelation 13:9-10:

> *"If any man have an ear, let him hear. He that leadeth into captivity shall go into captivity: he that killeth with the sword must be killed with the sword. Here is the patience and the faith of the saints".*

Now here is a more accurate "breakdown" of what the passage actually means:

REVELATION 13:9-10—MINI-BREAKDOWN

Context: John is describing war between the people of God and the Beast.

Main Point: A call for believers to remain faithful in the midst of persecution.

Breakdown: Verses 9-10 are a parenthetical warning to believers to listen and obey. It is a serious admonition to anyone who has an ear.

John's repeating of the command from the letters to the seven churches ties it into John's day, and not just the end times. Revelation 13:10 alludes to both Jeremiah 15:2 and Jeremiah 43:11. Within the book of Revelation itself, 13:10 harkens back to Revelation 2:10. Within the New Testament, Matthew 24:9, 21 and Matthew 26:52. During these events, Christians are called, not to take up arms but to remain faithful.

Ultimately, Yahweh will win this war so leave the battle to the LORD. The persecution is ordained by God and therefore ... "resistance is futile". But those who take up the sword against God's people will be judged. Therefore, the saints are to patiently endure their suffering. It is a word of comfort for the church.

A "Hebrew Israelite" may accept this understanding and "add it" to their own. He or she may feel this doesn't necessarily refute their understanding of these verses directly applying to Caucasians. A more nuanced "Hebrew Israelite" may agree these passages are definitely a warning to the people of God to remain faithful ... but they may say that does not void the commination to those who lead others into captivity - believers or not. (For these two paragraphs, I am reworking a post by "Vladimir Saintius", a former 1Wester who calls the 1West understanding of Revelation 13:9-10 a "chimerical interpretation".).

Recall: the standard 1West interpretation is that the white man led the children of Israel into captivity; therefore, the white man will also be led into captivity. But the men who were slave traders in the 1600s are dead; therefore, they cannot be led into captivity. 1Westers believe they will be reincarnated to receive judgment and to be slaves themselves. But since they believe they will lead the white man into captivity, wouldn't that mean they would also someday be led into captivity? The cycle would never end.

THE GOSPEL ACCORDING TO HEBREW ISRAELISM

Very few "Hebrew Israelite" works focus on the gospel (even a twisted one!) or discuss their understanding of biblical salvation in depth. In layman's terms, the soteriology of Hebrew Israelism is an absolute mess. The closes parallel are the Judaizers (*'Ιουδαΐζειν, Ioudaizein*) of Galatians 2:14. "Hebrew Israelites" are akin to modern day Harlem Judaizers, or Chicago Judaizers, or Dimona Judaizers. 1Westers only Judaize those they perceive to be fellow "Israelites", as 1Westers do not believe the so-called "other nations" have any chance of salvation.

The exception is GOCC – they Judaize everybody! Elder Shadrock Porter's Canadian-based "Israelite" group are not 1Westers, so their soteriology would match closer with GOCC (a 1West offshoot who began accepting so-called "other nations"). Still, I have found their writings on salvation to be illuminating. First, they actually have written on the subject in a relatively clear manner. This alone makes them stand out. Second, their words give full illustration of the Judaizing tendencies of all "Hebrew Israelite" groups:

> *Grace is that source that can save the world, but it is only given by an Israelite, because he is the rich man. He gets his riches by keeping the laws, the statutes and the commandments. The heathen and the Gentile would get their riches through him. In other words, the Israelites are always under the law, the law is their source. The Gentile would be under grace, because they are not of the circumcision, and they were not chosen by God.*[2]

The next page declares "we will prove that no one except an Israelite can gain salvation direct from God".[3] The page after interprets Ephesians 2:3-9:

> *... please do not generalize statements written in the Bible. They are strictly for, and about Israelites. In the third verse Paul is reminding the Gentiles who they really were, the children of wrath. In verses 7 and 8 we notice the clearness and clarity of the underlined statement that the Gentiles cannot be saved by themselves, but by the grace of the Christ who was an Israelite, and through faith. The only way a Gentile and an Israelite can join together in Christ, is through the doctrine of Israel – not Christianity.*[4]

THE GOSPEL FOR THE "HEBREW ISRAELITES"

If you have a basic, Sunday School level of understanding the Gospel, the quotes above will not make sense. You may even be able to break down the manifold problems in the soteriology. If not, let me share one more shocking statement from the same book. The author writes that "the song 'Amazing Grace'" is "strictly for Gentiles, and no Israelite should ever utter it".[5] What follows is not a complete breakdown of the true doctrine salvation; rather, it is a compilation of key Scriptures which you can share with a "Hebrew Israelite" friend. Studying and understanding these will shed light on the true Gospel of Jesus Christ as opposed to the Gospel of One West.

PRINCIPLE #1: THE GOSPEL IS OF SUPREME IMPORTANCE

Scripture 1: Romans 1:16

> *For I am not ashamed of* ***the gospel*** *of Christ: for it* ***is the power of God unto salvation*** *to everyone that believeth; to the Jew first, and also to the Greek.*

Scripture 2: 1 Corinthians 15:1–4

> **1** *Moreover, brethren, I declare unto you the* ***gospel which I preached*** *unto you, which also ye have received, and wherein ye stand;*
>
> **2** ***By which also ye are saved****, if ye keep in memory what I preached unto you, unless ye have believed in vain.*
>
> **3** *For I delivered unto you* ***first*** *of all that which I also received,*

how that ***Christ died for our sins according to the scriptures****;*

4 *And that he was buried, and that he rose again the third day according to the scriptures.*

PRINCIPLE #2: SALVATION IS NOT OF THE LAW BECAUSE NO ONE KEEPS THE LAW (OR: ALL SIN AND THIS REQUIRES JUDGMENT)

Scripture 1: Romans 6:23

For the wages of ***sin*** is ***death****; but the* ***gift*** *of God* is ***eternal life*** *through* ***Jesus Christ*** *our* ***Lord****.*

Scripture 2: Romans 3:23

For ***all have sinned****, and* ***come short*** *of the glory of God.*

Scripture 3: Romans 3:20

Therefore ***by the deeds of the law there shall no flesh be justified*** *in his sight: for by the law* is *the knowledge of sin.*

Scripture 4: Romans 9:30–33

What shall we say then? That the Gentiles, which followed not after righteousness, have attained to righteousness, ***even the righteousness which is of faith****. 31 But Israel,* ***which followed after the law of righteousness, hath not attained to the law of righteousness****. 32 Wherefore? Because* **they sought it** ***not by faith, but as it were by the works of the law****. For they stumbled at that stumbling stone; 33 As it is written, Behold, I lay in Sion a stumbling stone and rock of offence: and* ***whosoever believeth on him shall not be ashamed****.*

Scripture 5: Galatians 5:2–4

> **2** *Behold, I Paul say unto you, that* ***if ye be circumcised, Christ shall profit you nothing****.*
>
> **3** *For I testify again to every man that is circumcised, that* ***he is a debtor to do the whole law****.*
>
> **4** *Christ is become of no effect unto you,* ***whosoever of you are justified by the law; ye are fallen from grace****.*

Scripture 6: Galatians 6:13

> *For* ***neither they themselves who are circumcised keep the law****; but desire to have you circumcised, that they may glory in your flesh.*

Scripture 7: Isaiah 59:2

> *But* ***your iniquities have separated between you and your God, And your sins have hid*** his ***face from you****, that* ***he will not hear****.*

PRINCIPLE #3: THE OLD COVENANT POINTS TO CHRIST & THE NEW COVENANT

Scripture #1: Luke 24:25–27

> **25** *Then he said unto them, O fools, and slow of heart to believe* ***all that the prophets have spoken****:*

26 *Ought not Christ to have suffered these things, and to enter into his glory?*

27 *And* ***beginning at Moses and all the prophets, he expounded unto them in all the scriptures the things concerning himself****.*

Scripture #2: Luke 24:45–49

45 *Then opened he their understanding,* ***that they might understand the scriptures,***

46 *And said unto them, Thus it is written, and thus it behooved Christ to suffer, and to rise from the dead the third day:*

47 *And that* ***repentance and remission of sins should be preached in his name among all nations, beginning at Jerusalem****.*

48 *And ye are witnesses of these things.*

49 *And, behold, I send the promise of my Father upon you: but tarry ye in the city of Jerusalem, until ye be endued with power from on high.*

Scripture #3: Romans 4:2–4

2 *For* ***if*** *Abraham were justified by works, he hath whereof to glory; but not before God.*

3 *For what saith the scripture?* ***Abraham believed God, and it was counted unto him for righteousness****.*

4 *Now to him that worketh is the reward not reckoned of grace, but of debt.*

Scripture #4: Galatians 3:10–14

10 *For as many as are of the works of the law are under the curse: for it is written,* ***Cursed*** **is** ***every one that continueth not in all things which are written in the book of the law to do them.***

11 ***But that no man is justified by the law in the sight of God,*** **it is** ***evident: for, The just shall live by faith.***

12 ***And the law is not of faith:*** *but, The man that doeth them shall live in them.*

13 ***Christ hath redeemed us from the curse of the law,*** *being made a curse for us: for it is written, Cursed* is *every one that hangeth on a tree:*

14 *That* ***the blessing of Abraham might come on the Gentiles through Jesus Christ; that we might receive the promise of the Spirit through faith.***

PRINCIPLE #4: CHRIST FULFILLED THE LAW PERFECTLY AND CHRIST COMPLETELY PAID THE PENALTY FOR OUR SIN

Scripture #1: Romans 5:12–21

12 *Wherefore, as by one man sin entered into the world, and death by sin; and so death passed upon all men, for that* ***all have sinned:***

13 *(For until the law sin was in the world: but sin is not imputed when there is no law.*

14 *Nevertheless death reigned from Adam to Moses, even over them that had not sinned after the similitude of Adam's transgression, who is the figure of him that was to come.*

15 *But not as the offence, so also is the free gift. For if through the offence of one many be dead, much more the grace of God,* ***and the gift by grace,*** **which is** ***by one man, Jesus Christ, hath abounded unto many.***

16 *And not as* it was *by one that sinned,* so is ***the gift****: for the judgment was by one to condemnation, but the* ***free gift*** **is** ***of many offences unto justification.***

17 *For if by one man's offence death reigned by one;* ***much more they which receive abundance of grace and of the gift of righteousness shall reign in life by one, Jesus Christ.)***

18 *Therefore as by the offence of one* judgment **came** ***upon all men*** *to condemnation; even so* ***by the righteousness of one*** **the free gift** ***came upon all men unto justification of life.***

19 *For as by one man's disobedience many were made sinners, so* ***by the obedience of one shall many be made righteous.***

20 *Moreover the law entered, that the offence might abound. But where sin abounded, grace did much more abound:*

21 *That as sin hath reigned unto death, even so might* ***grace reign through righteousness unto eternal life by Jesus Christ our Lord.***

Scripture #2: Ephesians 2:8–10

> **8** *For* ***by grace are ye saved through faith****; and that* ***not of yourselves****:* it is *the* ***gift of God****:*
>
> **9** *lest any man should boast.*
>
> **10** *For we are his workmanship, created in Christ Jesus unto good works, which God hath before ordained that we should walk in them.*

Therefore, we are justified before God ***by grace alone***
on account of the work of ***Christ alone***
and this free justification is through ***faith alone***

PRINCIPLE #5: CHRIST USHERED IN THE NEW COVENANT

Scripture: Hebrews 7:11–24 (the priestly order is set aside)

> **11** *If therefore perfection were by the Levitical priesthood, (for under it the people received the law,) what further need* was there *that another priest should rise after the order of Melchisedec, and not be called after the order of Aaron?*
>
> **12** *For the priesthood being* ***changed****, there is made of necessity a* ***change*** *also of the law.*
>
> **13** *For he of whom these things are spoken pertaineth to another tribe, of which no man gave attendance at the altar.*
>
> **14** *For* it is *evident that our Lord sprang out of Juda; of which tribe Moses spake nothing concerning priesthood.*

15 *And it is yet far more evident: for that after the similitude of Melchisedec there ariseth another priest,*

16 *Who is made, not after the law of a carnal commandment, but after the power of an endless life.*

17 *For he testifieth, Thou* art *a priest for ever after the order of Melchisedec.*

18 *For there is verily a* ***disannulling*** *of the commandment going before for the* ***weakness*** *and* ***unprofitableness*** *thereof.*

19 *For* ***the law made nothing perfect, but the bringing in of a better hope*** did*; by the which we draw nigh unto God.*

20 *And inasmuch as not without an oath* he was made priest*:*

21 *(For those priests were made without an oath; but this with an oath by him that said unto him, The Lord sware and will not repent, Thou* art *a priest for ever after the order of Melchisedec:)*

22 ***By so much was Jesus made a surety of a better testament****.*

23 *And they truly were many priests, because they were not suffered to continue by reason of death:*

24 *But this* man, ***because he continueth ever, hath an unchangeable priesthood****.*

PRINCIPLE #6: OUR RESPONSE IS TO REPENT AND TRUST THE WORK OF CHRIST

Scripture #1: Romans 3:28

> *Therefore we conclude that **a man is justified by faith without the deeds of the law**.*

Scripture #2: Romans 10:9-13

> 9 *That if thou shalt **confess with thy mouth the Lord Jesus**, and shalt **believe in thine heart that God hath raised him from the dead, thou shalt be saved**.*
>
> 10 *For **with the heart man believeth unto righteousness**; and **with the mouth confession is made unto salvation**.*
>
> 11 *For the scripture saith, **Whosoever believeth on him shall not be ashamed**.*
>
> 12 *For there is no difference between the Jew and the Greek: for **the same Lord over all is rich unto all that call upon him**.*
>
> 13 *For **whosoever shall call upon the name of the Lord shall be saved**.*

PRINCIPLE #7: SALVATION IS FOR ALL THOSE WHO BELIEVE FROM EVERY NATION

Scripture: Acts 11:1-18

> 1 *And the apostles and brethren that were in Judaea **heard that the Gentiles had also received the word of God**.*

2 *And when Peter was come up to Jerusalem, they that were of the circumcision contended with him,*

3 *Saying, Thou wentest in to men uncircumcised, and didst eat with them.*

4 *But Peter rehearsed the matter from the beginning, and expounded it by order unto them, saying,*

5 *I was in the city of Joppa praying: and in a trance I saw a vision, A certain vessel descend, as it had been a great sheet, let down from heaven by four corners; and it came even to me:*

6 *Upon the which when I had fastened mine eyes, I considered, and saw fourfooted beasts of the earth, and wild beasts, and creeping things, and fowls of the air.*

7 *And I heard a voice saying unto me, Arise, Peter; slay and eat.*

8 *But I said, Not so, Lord: for nothing common or unclean hath at any time entered into my mouth.*

9 ***But the voice answered me again from heaven, What God hath cleansed, that call not thou common****.*

10 *And this was done three times: and all were drawn up again into heaven.*

11 *And, behold, immediately there were three men already come unto the house where I was, sent from Caesarea unto me.*

12 *And the Spirit bade me go with them, nothing doubting. Moreover these six brethren accompanied me, and* ***we entered into the man's house****:*

13 *And he shewed us how he had seen an angel in his house, which stood and said unto him, Send men to Joppa, and call for Simon, whose surname is Peter;*

14 *Who shall tell thee words, whereby thou and all thy house shall be saved.*

15 ***And as I began to speak, the Holy Ghost fell on them, as on us at the beginning.***

16 *Then remembered I the word of the Lord, how that he said, John indeed baptized with water; but ye shall be baptized with the Holy Ghost.*

17 ***Forasmuch then as God gave them the like gift as he did unto us, who believed on the Lord Jesus Christ; what was I, that I could withstand God?***

18 ***When they heard these things, they held their peace, and glorified God, saying, Then hath God also to the Gentiles granted repentance unto life.***

CHAPTER 5 ENDNOTES

1. WILLIS, J.R.. *THE PROPHECIES: The Book of the Hebrew Israelites* (Kindle Locations 12617-12632). Y.C.I.K PRODUCTIONS LTD.. Kindle Edition.

2. Shadrock, editor. *The Word The Israelites and the Damned.* (Toronto Ontario Canada: Fifth Rib Publishing, 1993), 99.

3. Shadrock, editor. *The Word The Israelites and the Damned.* (Toronto Ontario Canada: Fifth Rib Publishing, 1993), 100.

4. Shadrock, editor. *The Word The Israelites and the Damned.* (Toronto Ontario Canada: Fifth Rib Publishing, 1993), 101.

5. Shadrock, editor. *The Word The Israelites and the Damned.* (Toronto Ontario Canada: Fifth Rib Publishing, 1993), 102.

"This will be the best book you have ever read. Your history and religion wrapped in the pages of truth. Written in simple language. You ought to find out. Read it for yourself. The truth is a dangerous weapon and I hereby challenge anyone to prove it wrong."

–From the back cover of *The Word, The Israelites and The Damned*, edited by Canadian "Hebrew Israelite" leader, Shadrock.

RESOURCES TO STUDY "HEBREW ISRAELISM"

Currently, there are no publications on the modern 1West incarnation of Hebrew Israelism. No books deal with the recent upsurge in self-publishing, whether it is through books or online materials. No literature hashes out the distinctions amongst the different modern sects (only a few even mention 1West). No writings give an in-depth theological analysis or contextual gospel-based solutions.

Very few books deal with 1West claims directly. We must apply the truth in related books more directly to the issues raised by "Hebrew Israelites." There are no books which fully line up with the approach of a Christian apologist but there are books which are "support pegs." These books have helpful and relevant sections which we can aggregate together to marshal the church's current resources. This chapter includes a small bibliography to assist Christians as they research this group and their claims. I have gathered a sizable number of relevant resources: websites, video/audio resources, journal articles, dissertations, and books. I'll share some of them here.

"Hebrew Israelites" have unbiblical view of ethnic identity and it shows up in their bigoted attitudes. The following are excellent books for getting a biblical perspective on people groups, culture, and ethnicity: *From Every People and Nation* by J. Daniel Hays, *One New Man: Cross and Racial Reconciliation in Pauline Theology* by Jarvis Williams, and *Bloodlines: Race, Cross and the Christian* by John Piper. These books lay out a biblical anthropology, applying it to ethnic divisions in our world. They are helpful in understanding how the Bible (and therefore the Creator) views people and what that means for the church.

One Human Family: The Bible, Science, Race and Culture by Carl Wieland, *Shattering the Myth of Race: Generic Realities and Biblical Truths* by Dave Unander, and *One Race, One Blood: The Biblical Answer to Racism*, cover similar territory but add an additional help: science. These authors have a background in understanding creation and apply Scripture and science (such as genetics) to people groups. These are unique resources on the implied "Hebrew Israelite" claims about genetics.

The next three books touch on the same territory (genetics) but in a much more in-depth way. They are from non-Christians (and therefore contain some Darwinistic presuppositions) but are still stellar. *Legacy: A Genetic History of the Jewish People* by Harry Ostrer, *Abraham's Children: Race, Identity, and the DNA of the Chosen People* by Jon Entine, and *Jacob's Legacy: A Genetic View of Jewish History* by David B. Goldstein are secular academic works which give the science and genetic studies which – if properly synthesized and applied – will refute many "Hebrew Israelite" claims about Abraham's physical descendants. Since 1Westers claim Native Americans are Gad and Reuben, works on indigenous genetics are also helpful: *The Origins of Native Americans: Evidence from Anthropological Genetics*, by Michael H. Crawford, *Losing a Lost Tribe: Native Americans, DNA, and the Mormon Church* by Simon G. Southerton, and *American Apocrypha: Essays on the Book of Mormon*, edited by Dan Vogel and Brent Lee Metcalfe (Chapter 3).

Three standard (or they should be!) academic works in this field are *Chosen People: The Rise of American Black Israelite Religions* by Jacob S. Dorman, *Black Judaism: Story of an American Movement* by James E. Landing, and *Thin Description: Ethnography and the African Hebrew Israelites of Jerusalem* by John L. Jackson, Jr. They are published by Oxford, Carolina Academic Press, and Harvard, respectively. These works are excellent at giving the historical rise of these groups. The latter work even has four pages on "camps," giving the names of different sects and their separate local chapters.

There are no Christian books strictly on the "Hebrew Israelites." There are a few apologetic books which mention them: *Black Man's Religion: Can Christianity Be Afrocentric?* by Glenn Usry and Craig S. Keener, *Urban Apologetics: Why the Gospel is Good News for the City* by Christopher W. Brooks, and *The Round Table: A Christian's Conversation with Marginal Beliefs Affecting the Black Church Experience* by Rahsaan A. Armand and Tyran T. Laws. The demand is growing, let us pray and work to actualize the supply.

There are Christian books which touch on relevant subjects: the Sabbath Day; The Law; the African church; the black church in the US; bigotry; diversity, and ethnicity. Some helpful books in this regard are *The Blessing of Africa: The Bible and African Christianity* by Keith Augustus Burton; *Africa and the Bible* by Edwin M. Yamauchi; *Beyond Roots: In Search of Blacks in the Bible* and *Beyond Roots II: If Anybody Ask You Who I Am: A Deeper Look at Blacks in the Bible*, both by William Dwight McKissic, Sr.; *A History of Christianity in Africa: From Antiquity to the Present* by Elizabeth Isichei; *How Africa Shaped the Christian Mind: Rediscovering the African Seedbed of Western Christianity* by Thomas C. Oden, and *Africa and Africans in the New Testament* by David Tuesday Adamo.

There is a considerable amount on this subject by non-Christians, often by Jewish or black scholars. Some are helpful, none go deep into exegesis, and none offer spiritual answers. Hardly any deal with the current adherents who have gained strength the past few decades (the more militant groups who use street-style tactics and "do-it-yourself" methods more than their forebears). Here are some of this class of book: *The Church of God and Saints of Christ: The Rise of Black Jews* by Elly M. Wynia; *Brother Love: Murder, Money and a Messiah* by Sydney P. Freedberg; *Black Jews in Africa and the Americas*; *The Lost Tribes of Israel: The History of a Myth*, both by Tudor Parfitt; *The New Ship of Zion: Dynamic Diaspora Dimensions of the African Hebrew Israelites of Jerusalem* by Martina Koenighofer; *The Black Jews of Africa: History, Religion, Identity* by Edith Bruder; *African Zion: Studies in Black Judaism*, edited by Edith Bruder and Tudor Parfitt; *Judaising Movements: Studies in the Margins of Judaism* by Tudor Parfitt and Emanuela Trevisan Semi; *Black Zion: African American Religious Encounters with Judaism* edited by Yvonne Chireau and Nathaniel Deutsch, and *Black Jews in America: A Documentary with Commentary* by Graenum Berger.

WORKS FOCUSED ON BLACK OR URBAN CHRISTIANITY

Black and Tired: Essays on Race, Politics, Culture and International Development – Anthony B. Bradley (2011)

Black Man's Religion: Can Christianity Be Afrocentric? – Glenn Usry and Craig S. Keener (1996)

How Black is the Gospel? – Tom Skinner (1970)

Beyond Roots: In Search of Blacks in the Bible – William Dwight McKissic, Sr. (1990)

Beyond Roots II: If Anybody Ask You Who I Am: A Deeper Look at

Blacks in the Bible – William Dwight McKissic, Sr. and Anthony T. Evans (1994)

Black and Reformed: Seeing God's Sovereignty in the African-American Christian Experience – Anthony J. Carter (2016)

The Decline of African American Theology: From Biblical Faith to Cultural Captivity – Thabiti M. Anyabwile (2007)

Defending Black Faith: Answers to Tough Questions About African-American Christianity – Craig S. Keener and Glenn Usry (1997)

Free At Last? The Gospel in the African American Experience – Carl F. Ellis Jr. (1996)

Free Indeed: Heroes of Black Christian History – Mark Sidwell (2001)

Heroes in Black History: True Stories From the Lives of Christian Heroes – Dave and Neta Jackson (2008)

Introducing Black Theology: Three Crucial Questions for the Evangelical Church – Bruce L. Fields (2001)

Keep Your Head Up: America's New Black Christian Leaders, Social Consciousness, & The Cosby Conversation (2012) – Anthony B. Bradley, editor

Liberating Black Theology: The Bible and the Black Experience in America – Anthony B. Bradley (2010)

Profiles of African-American Missionaries – Robert J. Stevens and Brian Johnson (2012)

Reviving the Black Church – Thabiti Anyabwile (2015)

Setting the Record Straight: American History in Black & White – David Barton (2013)

Urban Apologetics: Why the Gospel is Good News for the City – Christopher W. Brooks (2014)

A BIBLICAL VIEW OF PEOPLES AND CULTURES

The Biblical Offense of Racism – Douglas Jones (2007)

Bloodlines: Race, Cross and the Christian – John Piper (2011)

Christ and the Dominions of Civilization – Love L. Sechrest (2009)

From Every People and Nation – J. Daniel Hays (2003)

One Human Family: The Bible, Science, Race and Culture – Carl Wieland (2014)

One New Man: The Cross and Racial Reconciliation in Pauline Theology – Jarvis Williams (2010)

One Race One Blood: The Biblical Answer to Racism – Ken Ham and A. Charles Ware (2010)

AFRICA IN THE BIBLE AND IN CHRISTIAN HISTORY

A History of Christianity in Africa: From Antiquity to the Present – Elizabeth Isichei (1995)

Africa and the Bible – Edwin M. Yamauchi (2004)

The Africana Bible: Reading Israel's Scriptures from Africa and the African Diaspora - Hugh R. Page, Jr. (2009)

The Blessing of Africa: The Bible and African Christianity – Keith Augustus Burton (2007)

How Africa Shaped the Christian Mind: Rediscovering the African Seedbed of Western Christianity – Thomas C. Oden (2012)

Jesus and the Gospel in Africa: History and Experience – Kwame Bediako (2012)

The Lost History of Christianity: The Thousand-Year Golden Age of the Church in the Middle East, Africa, and Asia – and How It Died – Philip Jenkins (2008)

HISTORICAL BACKGROUNDS OF THE ANCIENT NEAR EAST

After the Flood: The Early Post-Flood History of Europe Traced Back to Noah – Bill Cooper (1995)

Ancient Egypt and the Old Testament – John D. Currid (1997)

Ancient Israel in Sinai: The Evidence for the Authenticity of the Wildeness Tradition – James K. Hoffmeier (2011)

Ancient Post-Flood History: Historical Documents that Point to Biblical Creation – Ken Johnson (2012)

Egypt and Bible History: From Earliest Times to 1000 B.C. – Charles F. Aling (1981)

Israel and the Nations: From the Exodus to the Fall of the Second Temple – F.F. Bruce (1963)

Israel in Egypt: The Evidence for the Authenticity of the Exodus Tradition – James K. Hoffmeier (1996)

Peoples of the Old Testament World – Alfred J. Hoerth, Gerald L. Mattingly, Edwin M. Yamauchi, editors (1995)

Tower of Babel: The Cultural History of Our Ancestors – Bodie Hodge (2013)

Twelve Tribes of Israel – Jessica Curiel (2014)

UNDERSTANDING THE LAW AND THE OLD COVENANT

40 Questions About Christians and Biblical Law – Thomas R. Schreiner (2010)

Five Views on Law and Gospel – Stanley Gundry, editor (1999)

From Sabbath to Lord's Day – DA Carson, editor (1999)

What Do Jewish People Think About Jesus? And Other Questions Christians Ask about Jewish Beliefs, Practices & History – Michael L. Brown (2007)

UNDERSTANDING CULTIC RELIGIONS

Scripture Twisting: 20 Ways the Cults Misread the Bible – James W. Sire (1980)

Unmasking the Cults – Alan W. Gomes (1995)

BOOKS BY SECULAR OR NON-CHRISTIAN AUTHORS

Abraham's Children: Race, Identity, and the DNA of the Chosen People - Jon Entine (2007)

African-American Religion in the Twentieth Century: Varieties of Protest and Accommodation – Hans A. Baer and Merrill Singer (1992)

The African American Religious Experience in America – Anthony B. Pinn (2005)

African American Religious History: A Documentary Witness – Milton C. Sernett, editor (1999)

African American Religious Thought: An Anthology – Cornel West, Eddie S. Glaude, Jr. (2003)

Black Judaism: Story of an American Movement - James E. Landing (2002)

Black Gods of the Metropolis: Negro Religious Cults of the Urban North – Arthur Huff Fauset (1944)

Black Jews in Africa and the Americas – Tudor Parfitt (2013)

The Black Jews of Africa: History, Religion, Identity – Edith Bruder (2008)

*The Black Jews of Harlem: Negro Nationalism and the Dilemmas of Negro Leadership** – Howard M. Brotz (1964)

Black Atlantic Writers of the 18th Century: Living the New Exodus in England and the Americas – Adam Potkay and Sandra Burr, editors (1995)

Black Zion: African American Religious Encounters with Judaism - Yvonne Chireau and Nathaniel Deutsch (2000)

Brother Love: Murder, Money, and a Messiah – Sydney P. Freedberg (1994)

*Chosen People: The Rise of American Black Israelite Religions** – Jacob S. Dorman (2013)

The Church of God and Saints of Christ: The Rise of Black Jews – Elly M. Wynia (2014)

Dread Jesus – William David Spencer (1999)

The Heritage Seekers: Black Jews in Search of Identity – Israel J. Gerber (1977)

Islam and the Blackamerican: Looking Toward the Third Resurrection – Sherman A. Jackson (2005)

Israel in the Black American Perspective – Robert G. Weisbord and Richard Kazarian, Jr. (1985)

Jacob's Legacy: A Genetic View of Jewish History – David B. Goldstein (2008)

The New Black Gods: Arthur Huff Fauset and the Study of African American Religions – Edward E. Curtis and Danielle Brune Sigler, editors (2009)

The New Ship of Zion: Dynamic Diaspora Dimensions of the African Hebrew Israelites of Jerusalem - Martina Koenighofer (2008)

*Religion and the Racist Right: The Origins of the Christian Identity Movement** – Michael Barkun

Thin Description: Ethnography and the African Hebrew Israelites of Jerusalem – John L. Jackson, Jr. (2013)

Often, when I finish a book related to the subject, I go on Amazon and leave a mini-review. This as a public service of sorts: people looking into this will know what is good and what is bad, or at least they will have a warning or endorsement. People can also comment on Amazon reviews, so it is a way for adherents to engage me and defend or critique the book. In this section, I share a few of my adapted and revised mini-reviews.

FOUR MINI-SURVEYS

Black Judaism: Story of an American Movement – James Landing (2002)

Overall Summary: unique, one-of-a-kind resource

This book is an impressive feat. To study Hebrew Israelism, you must own this book. Landing has created a virtual encyclopedia, complete with regional and chronological breakdowns. The information Landing has compiled is absolutely essential, completely indispensable, and entirely fascinating.

It is textbook dry but its value outweighs its lack of style. A downside is its price tag. Still, it is a must have. Its only other weakness: it does not cover much of the 1West sect of Hebrew Israelism (that is where the "action" is).

Landing's work is a serious achievement for any scholar.

Chosen People: The Rise of American Black Israelite Religions – Jacob S. Dorman (2013)

Overall Summary: all-around excellence: compelling writing and important history

A must read for any student of Hebrew Israelism. Dorman uncovers important historical information. He does a stupendous job synthesizing data into a coherent whole. He aptly demonstrates interwoven ideological strands and common points of contact, such as black Wesleyans, Pentecostalism, and even Anglo-Israelism.

Dorman is clearly fascinated by the subject matter but manages to write in a relatively fair, objective, and even-handed manner. This helps the reader understand these movements with a certain level of empathy. Empathy is critical, especially when dealing with fringe offshoots some people may casually write off as "bizarre" or "weird".

This book does not give much information on the current wave of 1West "Hebrew Israelites." It will give the reader insight into where these movements came from but the 1West strand is less refined and more militant than the groups Dorman covers. Still, *Chosen People* is a key piece in the puzzle of understanding the picture of Hebrew Israelism.

Religion and the Racist Right: The Origins of the Christian Identity Movement – Michael Barkun (1997)

Overall Summary: A solid contribution to an inflammatory issue

I picked this up to learn how British-Israelism precedes and parallels Hebrew Israelism. Although the author does not mention Hebrew Israelism, the book does not disappoint. For example, much of the preface could be applied to 1West Hebrew Israelism.

Barkun's work is enlightening in its own right. For example, early 19th century Identity folks were into Pyramidism (like Charles Russell) and date setting (like Charles Russell). Some Identity adherents identified Egypt as the banking and financial system.

The criticism on Amazon reviews of this book is largely unwarranted. If I had to guess, it comes from ticked off "Anglo-Israelites" and their cohorts. The truth is, Barkun is relatively objective and usually fair to his subjects. Most importantly, he writes with respect and knowledge.

The Black Jews of Harlem: Negro Nationalism and the Dilemmas of Negro Leadership – Howard M. Brotz (1964)

Overall Summary: outdated but important slice of Harlem life

It's rare that an Amazon reviewer hits the nail on the head, but the review by user "Neurasthenic" is spot on. I second most of his sentiments (some with minor reservations):

> *A window into the Commandment Keepers in the mid-1960s. There were at one time about 3,000 black Jews in the United States and about 800 of them belonged to a movement called The Commandment Keepers, founded by Rabbi Wentworth Matthew. The first third of this book describes that movement, concentrating particularly on the shared rituals among congregation members, and how those evolved and were passed to new members. Brotz treats the organization mostly with respect though he includes some fairly absurd quotations from Matthew that I think were intended to elicit mirth in the reader. The final two-thirds of the book is a now dated rumination on the tension between assimilation and separatism in black politics, and to a lesser degree, how the example of the Commandment Keepers might inform our thinking on that topic.*

The quotes by Rabbi Matthew are relatively tame compared to many "Hebrew Israelite" leaders today. Current 1West groups like ISUPK, IUIC, and GMS are more unhinged than their predecessors. Their often meglomaniacal and uber-militant leaders frequently verbally war with each other over the most minuscule issues. The current crop of Harlem and NY-based camps make such grandiose and outlandish claims that Rabbi Matthew and his generation seem guarded and conservative by comparison.

This book is invaluable because of its up close narrative in those days - it gives a bird's eye view of the movement, circa 1964.

The last part of the book is a waste. Maybe it was considered by some to be mildly enlightened" for its time, but it is racially condescending, to say the least.

To the Reader: In the course of my research, I have uncovered many more books which are helpful for those entering into this mission field. Let me know (e-mail me at thestreetapologist@gmail.com) if you want me to share them with you. Also please let me know if you have suggestions to add to this list.

"One of the greatest obstacles an author who desires to write an urban apologetics text faces is the daunting task of composing a work that speaks to a dual audience. On the one hand, a book of this nature must make a reasonable attempt to honor the long tradition of Christian apologetics and those who have contributed to its growth and acceptance as a valuable field of study. This group has historically been, by and large, ethnically homogenous, having very little racial diversity. On the other hand, if an author expects an urban audience to become excited about his work, he must demonstrate the ability to connect on a more soulful level and not give in to the temptation to avoid addressing sensitive social issues. ... As ambitious as it may be to address a dual readership, the urban apologetics author, by necessity, must fully embrace this opportunity to be a true bridge builder".

-Christopher W. Brooks, *Urban Apologetics: Why the Gospel is Good News for the City*

"HEBREW ISRAELITE" BOOK SURVEY

Most books written from the "Hebrew Israelite" perspective are not professional but they do represent their beliefs on key matters. Many are self-published; some are only e-books. Other books are not "Hebrew Israelite" authors proper but are either friendly towards their positions or have been co-opted by the camps.

"Hebrew Israelite" authors range from non-1Westers – Ben Ammi's *The Power to Define: God, The Black Man and Truth* – to 1Westers – Tazadaq Shah's *The Real Hebrew Israelites vs Edom and Khazaria* – to those who blend 1West and non-1West theologies – *The Judahite's Hebrew Israelites for Dummies: The Family of Messiah*. The latter is poorly type-set and difficult to read. Many "Hebrew Israelite" works suffer from similar setbacks. Despite the extremely helter-skelter layout, it is a good thumbnail sketch of Hebrew Israelism.

The closest to a "Hebrew Israelite" "systematic theology" is *The Hebrew Israelite Manifesto* by a man who calls himself Prophet Travis Refuge.

It covers the big issues important to the modern "Hebrew Israelite" and includes a liberal dose of graphics, pictures and Internet memes – an extremely visual book.

Notable publications by "allied" authors are: *From Babylon to Timbuktu: A History of Ancient Black Races* by Rudolph R. Windsor and *We The Black Jews: Witness to the "White Jewish Race" Myth* by Yosef ben-Jochannan. Windsor and "Dr. Ben" (as he is affectionately called) give 1West members a basic (revised) vision of world history. Both books are somewhat dated and do not fully represent the movement's contemporary nuances. Both books are akin to "standard works" – these books are probably the most frequently recommended books on "Hebrew Israelite" affiliated websites – and many 1West members have read at least one.

A small, growing and important class of books are the all-too-brief memoirs by ex-members: *A Burden Has Been Lifted by Frede' Rica; Israel's Secret Cult: The Incredible Story of a Former Member of the African Hebrew Israelites of Jerusalem* by Mahaleyah Goodman; and *Why I Abandoned the Hebrew Israelite Religion* by Hannah Spivey.

BOOKS BY "HEBREW ISRAELITES"

An Authoritative Chronology of Hebrew Yisraelite: From Biblical Origins to Modern Times – Zebulon Hedeqyah (2015)

The Ancient Black Hebrews, Volumes I, II, III – Gert Muller

Art of the Ancient Black Hebrews – Djehuti Herakhuti (2014)

Black Bloodlines – Calvin Evans (2013)

The Black Hebrews and the Black Christ, Volumes I, II, III - Alymer Von Fleischer (2014)

The Black Madonna and Christ: What the Da Vinci Code Did Not Say - Gert Muller (2013)

The Black Role in the Bible – Alymer Von Fleischer (2013)

Embrace the Great Awakening: African American Women = Hebrew Israelite Women – Curtrice Gray (2013)

Hair Like Wool, Feet Like Burned Brass: The Color of Jesus and Burning Questions about the Messiah – Elisha Israel (2015)

Hebrews to Negroes: Wake Up Black America! – Ronald Dalton, Jr. (2015)

Hebrew Israelites for Dummies: The Family of Messiah – The Judahite (2015)

The Hidden Treasure the Lies in Plain Sight: The Truth about the So-Called Negros of America and the 12 Tribes – Jeremy Shorter (2014)

How Jesus Christ Became White – Alymer von Fleischer (2014)

Into Egypt Again With Ships: A Message to the Forgotten Israelites – Elisha Israel (2012)

Israel Unveiled – Brant Brown (2013)

The Jewish Masquerade: The Relationship Between Modern Jews and Ancient Hebrew-Israelites – John Brinson (2010)

The Power to Define: God, The Black Man and Truth – Ben Ammi (2015)

Scattered But Not Lost: History of the Hebrew Israelites – Ra Headley (2013)

Truth of Our Fathers: The Awakening of the Hebrew Israelites – F.A. Johnson (2014)

The Valley of the Dry Bones: The Conditions - Rudolphf R. Windsor

The Village of Peace, DVD (2015)

Wake Up To Your True Identity: Revealing the Biblical Identity of the so-called African-Americans – Maurice Lindsay (2015)

Yahushua the Black Messiah – Rabbi Simon Altaf (2013)

BOOKS BY "SYMPATHETIC" (OR CO-OPTED) AUTHORS

The Genesis of the Bible – Shaka Saye Bambata Dolo (2012)

"Go Tell My People Who They Are!" The True Biblical Identity of Black People – Janice Swinton (2011)

Hebrewisms of West Africa – Joseph J. Williams (1930)

Ibos: Hebrew Exiles from Israel – Onwukwe Alaezi (2013)

Lost Tribes and Promised Lands: The Origins of American Racism – Ronald Sanders (1978)

The Thirteenth Tribe: The Khazar Empire and Its Heritage – Arthur Koestler (1974)

We The Black Jews: Witness to the "White Jewish Race" Myth, Volumes I & II – Yosef A.A. ben-Jochannan (1993)

What Color Was Jesus? – William Mosley (1987)

BOOKS BY FORMER "HEBREW ISRAELITE" MEMBERS

A Burden Has Been Lifted – Frede' Rica (2008)

Israel's Secret Cult: the Incredible Story of a Former Member of the African Hebrew Israelites of Jerusalem – Mahaleyah Goodman (2013)

Why I Abandoned the Hebrew Israelite Religion: A Memoir/Self-Help Guide – Hannah Spivey (2015)

SEVEN MINI-REVIEWS

From Babylon to Timbuktu: A History of Ancient Black Races Including the Black Hebrews – Rudolph R. Windsor (1969)

Overall Summary: Fails to meet Junior College level academic standards

If a reader is highly susceptible to believing the "Hebrew Israelite" version of history prior to reading this work, it's possible they will find *From Babylon to Timbuktu* compelling. It is extremely difficult imagining a more objective reader being taken in by this book. So poorly researched, consistently incongruent, and viciously circular in its argumentation is this book that it's simply stunning.

"Source?" "Prove it!" "Evidence?" are the most common notes I wrote in the side margin. Whole paragraphs, whole pages, and whole sections are filled with a mind-numbing bombardment of "information" that is unprovable speculation or sheer fantasy. The flaws are self-evident

to any reader learned in critical thinking, basic historiography, and the rules of logic. Unfortunately, the book simply does not hold up to common academic standards. It does need to be PhD-level, but it should at least adhere to basic persuasive essay standards!

Windsor's failure to meet common undergrad standard is ironic; he clearly considers himself an authority on ancient history. He frequently casts "final judgment" on controversial matters, often relays his own pet hunches as if they have merit, and speaks of his research as if it is original, thorough, and sufficient. Windsor tosses around the phrases "scholars agree" and "scholars know" like candy at a parade. The scholars he does name are often non-specialists or have been dead for decades – even hundreds of years. Windsor never interacts with current research on subjects he addresses. Rarely, if ever, does Windsor interact with any serious counter-arguments to his proposals.

Nevertheless, for anyone wanting to learn about Hebrew Israelism, this book is essential reading. The fact that *From Babylon to Timbuktu* is vaunted as a classic by groups who adhere to the "American Black = Hebrew Israelite" thesis does not speak well of the movement's discernment.

The Valley of the Dry Bones: The Conditions That Face Black People in America - Rudolph R. Windsor (1988)

Overall Summary: 1/3 Important History, 1/3 Conspiracy Theory, 1/3 Hal Lindsey

Windsor's thought is important in understanding Hebrew Israelism. A professional historian or academic traversing through this book will be disappointed by its lack of rigor and self-awareness. However, compared to most works from the "Hebrew Israelite" theological and historical perspective, it is (relatively) one of the best. Reading this book is helpful to outsiders who grew up with means and privilege in understanding the "Hebrew Israelite" perspective. To gain the most from this book, simply read with an empathetic ear.

Windsor excels at laying out the struggle faced by black America. Windsor wrote in the 80s but sadly, not much has changed. Personally, I sense he writes from a sincere place: he desires to offer real solutions.

Nonetheless, this book deserves a critical beat down for its sloppy historiography. Windsor transforms massive speculation into established fact with the stroke of a pen. The first section is the best overall. After that, it gets wackier and wackier until he morphs into the "Hebrew Israelite" Hal Lindsey (page 145), complete with false prophecies of his own (see pages 137 and 141).

A final commendable point is that Windsor does include some real history. He deserves praise for shining a light on lesser known but significant aspects of black history. Sadly, many credible historians don't do their job popularizing these facts. Amateurs like Windsor fill in the gap, sometimes successfully, but often falling flat when it comes to facts.

The Jewish Masquerade: The Relationship Between Modern Jews and Ancient Hebrew-Israelites – John Brinson (2010)

Overall Summary: easy to read but a stack of conspiracy theories

The book's vantage point is semi-post-modern in its take on historical truth. The introduction gives the impression the author thinks his historical methodology is almost "secular." Perhaps the author's seminary training at a more theologically liberal school (San Francisco Theological Seminary) implanted in him pieces of a secularized worldview? Brinson may be unaware he has multiple assumptions which do not comport with each other. For example, he argues as if Scripture is a final authority … but then feels free to make his own revisions.

On page 1 Brinson declares, "This book is not intended to cause anyone or any group to feel denigrated or hated but is rather, an attempt to shed light on the appropriation by a people of another person's identity." But by page 86, he says "the white race" is "the planet's chief menace." That might make your "friendly neighborhood white man" feel both denigrated and hated. On page 90, Brinson writes that the white "menace began its destructive march in a southerly direction towards our black civilizations."

Pages 102-103 contain the most bizarre claims of all: Japheth "became entrapped behind mountains of solid ice" and "lost his melanin." Here are a few more paragraphs:

> *There is no way you can get melanin out of something it doesn't exist within but you can get white (paleness) out of black. This can be accomplished by diluting the black. The people who are defined as white are not white at all. They are merely translucent or, colorless and do not have access to a productive pineal gland that seems to play a major role in manufacturing melanin.*
>
> *Since sunlight was a rarity they had no use for melanin, which protects the skin from the sun's ultra violet rays, so they lost most of it and developed pale skin or albinism and etc. Eureka, the creation of the so-called white man occurred and he has evolved into an absolute menace to the planet and its other occupants.*

The book veers more conspiratorial as it moves along, with Chapter 5 "Where Did the Hebrew-Israelites Originate?" and Chapter 6 "The So-Called European/American Jew" being the most difficult to follow in their argumentation and the most wild in their accusations.

John Brinson strikes me as a genuine and sincere man but his book is not a trustworthy source. Instead it is an easy to refute stack of conspiracy theories, which, in the wrong hands, could be used to fuel hate.

Embrace the Great Awakening: African-American Women=Hebrew Israelite Women - Curtrice Gray

Overall Summary: poor writing, poor theology BUT you can feel the heart

Frankly, this book is shoddy. There are *major* problems in the author's biblical interpretation, formatting and grammar.

Based on the author's language, it seems she was raised in a "oneness" United Pentecostal Church environment, fell away for a spell, then became ensnared with Hebrew Israelism, and now believes she has found the truth. This book reads like the result of a theologically weak church that preyed on women instead of teaching them what it truly meant to be women of God.

Still, one can *feel* the author's heart in this work. She seems to be seeking. The astute reader can almost "sense" it. Her passion and intensity feel extremely raw and sincere.

What Color Was Jesus? – William Mosley (1987)

Overall Summary: Psychobabble+Liberation Theology+Sociological Pragmatism = *THIS*.

This book does very little to "demonstrate" that Jesus was black, yet it continually asserts it as fact. The author writes in the vein of a theologically liberal liberation theologian, rather than a biblical scholar or historian, emphasizing sociology and especially psychology. Ultimately, its aim seems pragmatic rather than historical, making it of little use for answering the question posed in its title.

Hair Like Wool, Feet Like Burned Brass: The Color of Jesus and Burning Questions about the Messiah – Elisha Israel (2015)

Overall Summary: better than most; still saddled with unbiblical bigotry

One of the best "Hebrew Israelite" books on the market. The author is more careful and argues more cogently than most of his peers.

For example, he stays away from the outlandish claims in the Sacred Name Movement. Not to say this is an academically rigorous book, but it does have some depth.

Sans the overemphasis on skin tone, the author's Christology seems nigh orthodox at points (e.g., on redemption and atonement). There are ambiguities in how the author discusses the incarnation but the author has a generally acceptable view of the Trinity. Much of the typology for the feasts and OT themes is basically sound (NOTE: I attempt to read each book with fresh eyes, judge it on its own merit, and be charitable in my interpretation. If I am incorrect in my understanding here, please forgive me).

The weaknesses come from retrojecting the author's perception of blackness onto the ancient Hebrews and Jesus. The author assumes - but never demonstrates - the tenet that black Americans are descendants of the Lost Tribes of Israel. Lastly, the author is saddled with an un-Christian bigotry towards those he sees as outside the Nation of Israel.

The Truth About Black Biblical Hebrew-Israelites (Jews): The World's Best-Kept Secret! – Ella J. Hughley (1982)

Overall Summary: lacks proper discernment in both sources and doctrine

A major problem with many "Hebrew Israelite" friendly books is a super sloppy use of sources. This book is no exception: Hughley cites dictionaries and encyclopedias as if they prove his point (e.g., pages 47, 56), yet doesn't always cite the publishing information. For example, page 39 merely says, "See *The New Compact Bible Dictionary*".

Hughley also relies on faulty sources. The most notable: Windsor's historically weak and academically anemic *From Babylon to Timbuktu*. The most egregious: Henry Ford's racist *The International Jew: The World's Foremost Problem*. Hughley categorizes it as an "in-depth study" (page 48). Ford's "study" pedigree is dubious: he was apparently the only American mentioned in *Mein Kampf* and *International Jew* is said to have influenced Hitler.

Not only does the author lack discernment in regards to sources, but also in regards to theology. The book is anti-Trinitarian (see page 57) and anthropocentric (man-centered ad opposed to God-centered). On page 54, the author writes "Man's greatest need is to discover the spiritual power which is within him." This is neither gospel nor the truth, despite the book's title.

I took extended quotes from Ella J. Hughley's *The Truth About Black Biblical Hebrew-Israelites (Jews): The World's Best-Kept Secret!* to give the reader a strong sense of its contents as well as a representation of "Hebrew Israelite" writing:

> *"This book is not at all intended to convey a racial or prejudicial point of view." (page 7)*

> *"We know that Abraham was black because he was born in the city founded by the black Nimrod, the grandson of Ham" (Gen. 10:8-10). page 11*

"The Bible dictionary defines Ham, Cush, and Nimrod as black men". (page 11)

"Moses had to be of the black race because he spent forty years in Pharaoh's palace among the black Egyptians, passing as Pharaoh's grandson. In order for him to have 'passed' as Pharaoh's grandson, he had to have looked just like the Egyptians among whom he lived. (Also, see Exodus 2: 18-19, where the people referred to Moses as an Egyptian.) One of the signs that God gave to Moses was when he turned his hand white. (Exodus 4:6-7). Had he been of the white race, what would have been the miracle of his hand turning white? The picture to be drawn from that incident is that the hand of a black man is turned white." (page 12)

"Jesus was also black, although the white religious institutions have portrayed him as white. Consider the following reference in the New Testament: "When Jesus came into the coast of Caesarea Philippi, he asked his disciples, saying, 'Whom do men say that I the Son of Man am?' And they said, 'Some say that thou art John the Baptist: some, Elias; and others, Jeremias, or one of the prophets.'" (Matt. 16:13, 14.) Here Jesus was compared with all of the prophets of old." (page 12)

"The foregoing information substantiates that the Israelites in the prop of the Bible were of the black race. All of them were descendants of Abraham, Isaac and Jacob." (page 13)

"Jesus as a prophet thought it was his responsibility to gather his fellow Israelites and return them to God through his teachings. He taught men and women to obey the Ten Commandments, love each other, and show kindness to all mankind, as had the prophets before him." (page 20)

"It is my belief that the foregoing prophecies, the prophecy of Ezekiel chapter 37 and many others began their modern – day fulfillment in 1896, when a prophet of the Almighty God, William Saunders Crowdy, resurrected and re-establish the house of Israel in Lawrence, Kansas." (page 29)

"Since its inception, many other smaller Black Hebrew Israelites come creations have sprung up. And though there may exist some areas of minor disagreement and plateaus of slight variance, they do agree on all basic tenets of faith, and recognize that they are the remnant of Israel descended from the Biblical tribes." (page 29)

"Jesus, speaking to the Pharisees, said, "Other sheep I have, which are not of this fold: them also I must bring, and they shall hear my voice; and there shall be one fold, and one shepherd. (John 10:14, 16). (See also Isaiah 56:6–8; Ezekiel 34:23.) Jesus is explaining in the foregoing quotation that there are other pure–hearted people (Gentiles) besides the Hebrew – Israelites (Jews) who will be brought together into the true house of Israel to worship God according to His commandments." (page 33)

"The white European Jews are descended from Esau, the brother of Jacob. These are the people referred to in Revelation 2:9 and 3:9." (page 35)

"Prior to the 17th century less emphasis was placed on race and/or color. In the 17th century Johan Frederich Blumenbach was the first to divide mankind according to skin color. Prior to this time the people were named after the country in which they lived, i.e., the name was equated with the country." (page 36)

"Eau is therefore described in the Bible as a ruddy (red), hairy man. This describes the 'white' man; he is red and hairy. ... The New Compact Bible Dictionary defines the word 'ruddy' as a word used to refer to 'a red or fair complexion', in contrast to the dark skin of the Hebrew. Esau is the white brother of Jacob, the father of the black Israelites." (page 39)

"Esau also took his wives of the daughters of Canaan;" (Gen. 36:2 – 3). (page 40)

"A decisive change in the relations between the two nations took place in the days of John Hyrcanus (end of the second century B.C.E.). Hyrcanus conquered the whole of Edom and undertook the forced conversion of its inhabitants to Judaism (Jos. Ant. 13:257ff).. Thence forth the Edomites became a section of the Jewish people, even becoming one of the ordinary administrative districts of the Hasmonean state. It appears that the Hasmonean dynasty used some of the respected families of Edom to establish its dominion in that country." (page 43)

"The Edomites are referred to in the Bible as the rich Jews. (See Rev. 2:9.) (page 45)

"This territory from India to Ethiopia was comprised of black people such as the Hittites, Hivites, Jebusites and Canaanites. Esau's descendants were Ishmaelites, Canaanites, Hittites and Hivites. These people of the black race intermarried with Esau of the white race, as indicated previously." (page 46)

"The Bible informs us that some of the Jews did not believe in Jesus's teachings and that they showed hostility toward him. Those who believed were no doubt the ones of Israelite ancestry; while those who hated him were offspring of Esau." (page 47)

"Genetically, they [the Khazars] are more closely related to Hun, Uighur and Magyar tribes than to the seed of Abraham, Isaac and Jacob." (page 48)

"Henry Ford, Sr., stated in his in-depth study entitled The International Jew (speaking about the white Jews as we know them today), that they are not the Old Testament people." (page 35)

"Juan Comas' contribution to the (UNESCO) series of booklets in Race and Science (pp. 33-35) entitled Racial Myths, states that ... 'It would be interesting to know the racial characteristics of the Hebrews of antiquity who are probably the main ancestors of the Jews of today; so far however, it has not been possible to ascertain them and thus it becomes necessary to conduct the investigation along other lines. ...'" (pages 49-50)

"Man's greatest need is to discover the spiritual power which is within him." (page 54)

Jesus "taught the belief in one God, and not the Trinity" (page 57)

"He clarified his mission as a prophet of God and not as a savior of the world. (Luke 13:33; Matthew 13:57; 4:24. Other biblical references include Luke 7:16; 24:19.) The prophets taught that God alone is our Savior. (Isaiah 60:16; Hosea 13:4)." (page 58)

"Jesus did not teach that he created the world. God created the world by himself, according to Isaiah 44:24; 40:12–18.) (page 58)

"It is possible that many of the Jews who did not believe in Jesus' teachings and hated him were of Esau– Edom, and the ones that believed were the ones of Israelite ancestry." (page 58)

"Jesus never said that he could save us from our sins." (page 59)

"The Savior – God concept is based on Egyptian and Babylonian religious rituals, which God condemned." (page 59)

"Some scholars writing on the origin of Christianity show how Christianity parallels with the Osirian religion; that the story of Osiris (one of the oldest Egyptian gods) appears in the four Gospels of the New Testament as being the story of Jesus the Christ. I, too, agree that the similarity is apparent." (page 59)

CONCLUSION

I wrote this brief publication because providing germane apologetic materials assists Christians in their apologetic, evangelistic, and discipleship efforts in the city and beyond. Studying the "Hebrew Israelite" movement equips Christians to better understand both Christianity and "Hebrew Israelism". Access to information about Hebrew Israelism is in demand but the supply is low. The final, complete, and expanded version of this pre-release abridged booklet will be one more brick in the wall of apologetic resources. This is why I wrote *Barack Obama vs. The Black Hebrew Israelites.*

Dear brothers and sisters in Christ, we need to put an end to this famine of resources. The Spirit will empower Christ's people for the task. Will we be vigilant and obedient? Or we will wilt away into the shadows of complacency and irrelevancy? God forbid! Consider this an urgent invitation for God's people to begin standing in the gap. Upload the videos, write the articles, conduct the interviews, record the podcasts, publish the books, craft the Power Points, and give the lectures! Now! Let us pray for men and women who are called to study this trend, learn how to explain it to others, and then passionately teach others how to refute the doctrines of Hebrew Israelism.

Love compels the Christian apologist to protect and prepare the vulnerable. Love compels us to become adept at giving practical answers to the questions "Hebrew Israelites" ask. For far too long, there has been a lack of attention paid to issues relating to urban apologetics. The time is now for deep, vibrant, and active Christian love to change the narrative ... and watch the Lord transform our cities for God's glory!

Soli deo Gloria!

VOCAB MALONE